Jonny Gumbel is one of the m
I know. The message of this bo
and preached over many years.
desperately we all need to kno
God – but I also welcome Jonny
Scripture but in the book of Romans, this message is substantive and
convincing, carrying the weight of Scripture in a way that anecdotal
explorations of a similar theme never can. It is a chaotic age and I find
my soul longing more and more for the shelter of God's love and the
anchorage of his word. I can't think of a better person to articulate this
message in precisely this way.

PETE GREIG
Founder of 24-7 Prayer International and Senior Pastor of Emmaus Rd Church,
Guildford

Jonny's hallmark humour is revealed through the mundane minutiae
of ordinary life, presenting a clear case that our need to be loved and to
love has already been met, and is waiting for us to receive. Its accessible
simplicity doesn't diminish the deep analysis of this life-changing love,
and what helps or hinders our experience of it.

SAMARA LEVY
Author of *Rebuilding the Ruins* and CEO of Samara's Aid Appeal

Loved is an incomparably clear and fantastically fluent meditation on
the central theme of book of Romans – of the profound power of the
love of God. Jonny Gumbel does his awesome subject justice ...

JAMES MUMFORD
Author of *Vexed: Ethics Beyond Political Tribes*

Jonny captures something wonderful in these pages, revealing the glory of God's love ... he writes in a way that is accessible, which elicited in me a desire to both read on and also to celebrate all that God has done. I heartily recommend this book.

REVD RUSSELL WINFIELD
Dean, St Mellitus College

It's great that someone at a St Peter's church should write a book inspired by St Paul! Like Peter and Paul, Archie Coates and Jonny Gumbel have also been partners in the Gospel, and this book emerges from their amazingly fruitful ministry in Brighton. God has given Jonny many gifts: the unfolding of profound truth in simple terms is one of them. This book started life as Sunday sermons that speak to every aspect of our life and times. It will make you laugh and cry as it makes connections with faith in Jesus Christ that take you by surprise. How does Mr Incredible get a mention, alongside George Eliot and Martin Luther King?

The first Apostles faced incredible challenges: today's Apostles still do. Loved is an affirmation of our condition of service; it is a gift for this generation.

THE RT REVD MARTIN WARNER
Bishop of Chichester

LOVED

LOVED

Jonny Gumbel
Foreword by Archie Coates

Knowing the love of God and how that
changes absolutely everything

Muddy
Pearl

Published in 2022 by

Muddy Pearl, Edinburgh, Scotland.

www.muddypearl.com

books@muddypearl.com

British Library Cataloguing in Publication Data

A catalogue record for this book is available from the British Library

ISBN 978-1-914553-12-7

Typeset in Minion by Revo Creative Ltd, Lancaster

Printed in Great Britain by Bell & Bain Ltd, Glasgow

Show me the wonders of your great love
PSALM 17:7

FOREWORD: *LOVED*

I confess to feeling a little uncertain when Jonny picked out the first few verses in Romans and announced he was starting a preaching series for the church, grinning that he wasn't quite sure when he'd be finished. Romans is wonderful of course, but strong meat, and I wasn't sure how we'd all cope.

Over ten years, Jonny and I shared most of the preaching Sunday by Sunday at St Peter's, Brighton. Sometimes we took a theme or book in the Bible and divvyed it up between us; but I quicky realized that the greatest impact seemed to come when Jonny was simply released to preach whatever God laid on his heart for our community in a particular season, and I tagged along filling in with bits and pieces.

In the event, Jonny preached through Romans once a month over three years, and it transformed our church. We became a more secure-in-Christ, light-hearted, purposeful and loving community.

Greeting church members on Sunday mornings, I would be asked, 'Is Jonny preaching today?', with my response eliciting either elation (and relief) or a brave 'well never mind, let's make the most of it' kind of expression in the face of disappointment. His unique ability to help every kind of person – whatever their age, background, intellectual ability or Christian experience – understand and apply theology, bringing the Bible alive and showing its relevance to every part of life, changed our church family and the non-churchgoing friends they brought along.

I am delighted therefore that Jonny has gone to the trouble of using what he preached as a basis for this precious book, so you too can benefit from his insights and wisdom. Please understand, these chapters are not a transcript of the sermons he delivered, as some books are. For a start, that would be quite impossible because much to my awe (and envy), Jonny preaches without notes. But more importantly, Jonny is an 'organic' communicator: he speaks and writes as a fellow pilgrim, moving through life with an open heart, humbly figuring out stuff as he goes along. Sermons were still in the process of being written moments before he stood up to deliver them, not because he was disorganized and started them late, but because he'd started them early and was still marvelling at the insights God gave him and working out how best to pass them onto the rest of us. Likewise, this book has been worked on over countless rewrites and edits, so that we can understand and grab hold of the marvellous truth that we are loved by God.

Jonny's great achievement here is to make the book of Romans accessible, and the love of God fresh, his clear explanation helped by a wonderful array of profound, touching and very amusing illustrations. Here we have biblical truth applied and relatable with the help of references to social science, history, literature, film, sport and family life. From Karl Barth to a story about sewage (I'll let you find that one), there really is something for everyone.

The quality of our lives is determined by how much we know we are loved by God. Our challenge is not the theory of this – we've heard 'God loves you' so often it's almost a cliché. Our challenge is to know deep down in our hearts that God loves us, so that it overflows and makes all the difference. The love of God is not something to believe once and then move onto other things. The love of God is what we feed on our whole lives long. May the Holy Spirit enlarge your understanding and ignite your heart as you read these chapters.

One tip. This is a book to take your time with. Let God speak to you as you read. Its bite-sized format is to be savoured more than consumed, and I have found it helpful to write my reflections into a journal as I go along, to more properly process and absorb. As I've done this, I've discovered a greater awe, richer joy and deeper inspiration to live well.

Archie Coates
Vicar Designate, Holy Trinity Brompton
2022

ACKNOWLEDGEMENTS

I will always be grateful to Archie and Sam Coates: for including Tara and me on their adventure to Brighton in 2009, for letting me take three years to preach through Romans about the love of God, and then repeatedly encouraging me to write this book.

To all those who helped me with this book. To Ali Verheul for turning twelve hours of talks into the start of a manuscript. To Tobias and Hannah Lancaster, Martin and Anna Smith, Steve and Jodi Luke and Terry and Maria Scard for providing prayer-filled and often snack-filled spaces for me to write in. To those who read the manuscript in the early stages and gave me feedback: Keir Shreeves, Sam Stephens, Phil Gladwin, Henry Gumbel, Archie Coates. To Chris Tilling for helping me with my theological questions. To Robyn Butler for drawing the diagrams for me and to James Mumford for doing his best to teach me how to write. And to Stephanie for reading the manuscript, being willing to publish it and for being enormously encouraging from start to finish.

Finally, I want to thank all those who have taught me about God's love through the years, particularly Mum and Dad (who instilled in me a confidence in a God who loved me from the very beginning), Becs (who inspired me that God's love enables us to be brave), Benj (who always insisted that God's love makes everything possible and therefore that every problem has a solution), Henry (who has never let me forget that every solution is itself also a problem and that God's love secures us enough to ask the most difficult questions) and Luigi (who inspired me that God's love is enough and worth giving up everything for and who pointed me in the right direction when I most needed it). And, of course, to Tara, and Albie, Titus, Iscah and Ettie for loving me and allowing me to love them, and for teaching me more than I can express about what it means to be loved. To those who had heard that I was writing a book on 'The

Romans' rather than Paul's letter to the Romans, I would like to apologize for the disappointment. Maybe next time.

CONTENTS

PROLOGUE

You are loved. Specifically, you are loved *by God*. (You may be loved by lots of other people, or no one, but you are certainly loved by God.) This is the most important thing about you. It is the answer to the deepest longings of your heart and has the potential to change your whole life in every possible way.

Our first and most fundamental need is to be loved. We arrive in this world needing to be wanted and cared for, and then as we grow up we want to be accepted and affirmed. We seek companionship and intimacy. We fear loneliness and isolation. In some ways our whole lives could be described as a search for love.

And in many ways, and for many people, there is a lot of love around us. Parents, partners, friends, even strangers. And yet our experiences of love – even the best ones – are always somehow inadequate. Even the best parents don't love us perfectly. No group of friends, or romantic relationships or level of popularity ever seems to be enough.

Christianity claims to have the answer to this problem. For Christians have always believed that at the heart of the Christian faith is the belief that God loves you and me. We hold that this is the message of the Bible. And that God's love for us is the solution to our search for love, that whether we know it or not, we are all looking for this divine love. Human love is a beautiful thing, but it does not compare to being loved by God, for human love is always imperfect, partial and temporary, whereas being loved by God means that we are loved perfectly, totally and eternally.

Christians claim that the proof of this love is found in the life of Jesus, and particularly through his death on the cross. We hold that the crucifixion of Jesus is a sign of God's love, and the definition of what it means to love. And that the Holy Spirit gives us a personal experience of this love. So, this is a love which is apparently both demonstrated and felt, which is known in our hearts and in our minds.

But what does it really mean for God to love us? And what difference does it make to our lives? What should we do about it?

This book is my attempt to answer these questions. It's a book about what it means to be loved by God: the nature of this love, the consequences of this love and our response to this love. If you're already a Christian, this is an attempt to describe this love that you have begun to experience. If you're not yet a Christian, this is what is on offer if you choose to put your faith in Jesus. I highly recommend it.

Although the whole of the Bible speaks of the love of God, I'll try to describe this love by looking at just one book, Paul's letter to the Romans, and what it teaches us about the love of God.

The Apostle Paul was one of the first Christians, someone whose life had been turned upside down by an experience of the love of God. He started a number of churches across the Roman Empire and wrote lots of letters to these churches and to others which he hadn't founded. Romans is his longest letter, and many would say his most important in terms of the impact it has had through the centuries.

We will work our way through it, following the order of the letter, starting at the first verse and finishing with the last, but there will be plenty that I skip over. This is definitely not an attempt to write a book about Romans. (As my father helpfully pointed out to me, 'There are already some very good books on Romans,' and I would recommend reading some of them.) Instead, it is a book about the love of God, and what the book of Romans might have to teach us about this love.

I have very few qualifications to write this book. I've studied a little theology, but I'm not a theologian. Once a month for three years I preached on this letter at St Peter's, Brighton, but I am certainly not an expert on the book of Romans, and there is a lot of it that I still don't understand. I have not done anything very impressive in my life thus far, apart from marrying someone 'out of my league' and having four children. And I'm certainly not a writer, coming from a family that competes as to who is the most dyslexic, and indeed wouldn't know how to spell 'dyslexic' without some help. My only qualification is that I am one who is, like the Church in Rome, 'loved by God', and I've been trying to live in this love for most of my life. These are a few things that I've been learning along the way.

So, let's start, as Paul does in his letter, with the question of your identity. For the first thing that God's love means is that you can know who you are.

Chapter 1

IDENTITY

... to all in Rome who are loved by God

ROMANS 1:7

'Now that we know who you are ... I know who I am. I'm
not a mistake! It all makes sense.'*

ELIJAH PRICE

You are loved by God. This is who you *are*. It is your identity.

Being a Christian is not just about what you think, though
it involves the transformation of our minds. It is not only about
what you feel, though it involves an experience of God himself.
Nor is it about what you do, though it radically alters the way you
live. It is not even about the group to which you belong, though
it redirects and reshapes your relationships. Being a Christian is
about something even more fundamental than this: it is about your
identity. It redefines who you are.

Socially, nationally, politically, we are always needing to address
questions of identity. And individually, we are all trying to work
out who we are. We can find ourselves forging our identity on any
number of things from our race, our politics, to our relationship
status. Or we might define ourselves based on our personality, our
sexuality, or our work or the opinions of others. Some markers are
external – our relationships, roles within a community, our culture.
Others can be internal – our desires, ambitions, character.

* *Unbreakable*, directed by M. Night Shymalan, Touchstone
Pictures, 2000.

Our attempts to define our identity are often based on comparisons, which can lead to pride or insecurity (if we define ourselves above or below other people), or division and hostility (if we define ourselves against the people around us).

And these various identities are often fragile. If we put our identity in being clever, and then fail an exam or say something stupid, then we lose our sense of self. If we put our identity in our work and then lose our job, we suddenly find we don't know who we really are any more.

This tendency to place our identity in something fragile is illustrated in J.R.R. Tolkien's *The Lord of the Rings*, where the evil Sauron pours all his power, malice and self into one ring, so that if that ring is destroyed, so is he. In similar ways, we can find ourselves pouring ourselves into our work, or a relationship, a project, or an image of ourselves to such an extent that if it were to be taken away, we would find that there was nothing left of us.

I found myself forced to deal with this question of identity in my early twenties. After feeling particularly tired over a long period, I discovered some lumps in my neck, which turned out to be evidence of glandular fever. No matter how much rest I had I didn't seem to feel any better. After a few months I was diagnosed with chronic fatigue syndrome, or ME. I had to drop out of university, stopped seeing any friends or playing sport, and for about a year did very little other than lie in bed hoping I would eventually recover. It was a time of intense confusion (because I couldn't work out what was going on), frustration (because I couldn't see the friends I wanted to see, read the books I wanted to read, or do any of the things I loved doing), and anxiety (because I couldn't see how this would ever end).

At a real low point in this period a friend (who is a Benedictine monk) came to see me. We walked a little through the streets near my home, and then, exhausted, I sat on the pavement to get some rest, feeling close to despair. He looked at me kindly, and then suddenly said, 'I'm glad this is happening to you, Jonny.' This didn't seem to be the most sensitive or encouraging thing to say. But then he continued to say that he thought that this was going to be an important period of my life. Then he looked at me again and said, 'You do not know who you are, but you are about to find out.'

He was right. During those painful months I was confronted by this vital question: who am I when all the normal markers of my identity have been taken away? If I am without my friends, or my studies, or my hobbies, or my health, who am I?

I began to realize that I had a choice. Either my identity would become my illness, which I knew would be disastrous, or it could be the one thing that no illness or disappointment could ever take away from me, which was that I was loved by God.

This was the life-changing revelation that emerged during that time. It wasn't dramatic or sudden. It emerged slowly, but consistently, in my heart and mind as I tried to listen to the voice of God over those months of doing almost nothing. The answer to the question of who am I if everything was taken away, was this: I am one who is loved by God.

Paul's letter to the Romans starts, like any other letter in the ancient world, with the question of identity. It begins by establishing who it's from and who it's to. At that time the standard formula for a letter would have been to have the name of the person writing the letter, then the name of the person or group it's written to, followed by a greeting. 'Paul, to the Church in Rome, greetings' would have been a perfectly adequate way to begin.

But the opening of this letter is unusually long, because Paul wants to communicate a few different things, one of which is to redefine the identity of those who were part of the Church in Rome. He addresses them very simply, 'To all in Rome *who are loved by God* and called to be saints' (1:7).

Paul could have mentioned all kinds of things about the Christians living in the capital of the most powerful empire the world had ever known. He could have addressed them as the world rulers, law-makers, those at the centre of culture, power and civilization. Alternatively, he could have addressed them as those in a city known for cruelty, violence, corruption and immorality. But for Paul the most important things about them are not their achievements or failings, their strengths or weaknesses, but that they are loved by God. They are in Rome, but they are not defined by Rome; they are defined by being loved by God.

This was true for the Church in Rome. It was true for me lying in bed unable to do anything. And this is true for you too. You are loved by God and this is the fundamental building block of your identity.

The love of God is so significant that it not only changes the way you think, feel and behave, but also changes your very identity. The love of God shows you who you are. You are not defined by your past, or your family, or your personality, or your sexuality, or your gender, or your job, or your marital status, or by your friends or the opinion of other people; you are defined by being loved by God. Descartes famously said, 'I think therefore I am,' but to be a Christian is one who knows, 'I am loved therefore I am.'

Knowing this secures us and sets us free. It is unshakeable. For whether you succeed or fail, whether people reject you or accept you, you are loved by God. You do not need to compare yourself or compete with others. You don't need to prove yourself or pretend to be something you're not. You don't need to try to impress anyone.

So many of the other markers of our identity are there to define us in contrast to other people, to explain our difference, or our superiority. And many of the world's conflicts have been caused by antagonism which has its roots in the question of identity. But this identity is one that unites. Paul was writing to a community that was divided along racial lines (Jews and Gentiles), but here was an identity that brought these two groups of Christians together.

Whether they were Jewish or Gentile, male or female, slave or free, they were loved by God.

The process of coming to know this love is often uncomfortable. God wants you to know this love which shapes your identity, so there may be times when he deliberately challenges or removes the things which you've held on to as the markers of our identity up till then. This is what God seemed to be doing during my time of illness. Having put my identity in all kinds of unhelpful things, God removed them one by one so that I might know that I was simply one who was loved by God. I might not be doing anything, seeing anyone, achieving anything, but I knew that I was loved by God.

The journey of the Christian life is one in which our identity becomes more and more defined by the love of God. The author of John's Gospel, writing near the end of his life and recording the stories of his three years with Jesus as a disciple before Jesus ascended into heaven, never refers to himself by his name. He mentions the other disciples by name, but the author, who seems to have had a particularly close relationship with Jesus, simply refers to himself as 'the disciple whom Jesus loved.'* Here was an Apostle, a leader of the early Church, one of the key eyewitnesses of Jesus' life and death and resurrection, and yet for him the only thing that mattered about himself was that he was loved by God.

So the love of God is the starting point for discovering who you are. But there is another element of these opening lines of Romans that is worth noticing, which is how Paul introduces himself. Normally one would state one's name and credentials, but Paul gets sidetracked. He writes:

Paul, a servant of Christ Jesus, called to be an apostle and set apart for the gospel of God – the gospel he promised beforehand through his prophets in the Holy Scriptures regarding his Son, who as to his earthly life was a descendant of David, and who through the Spirit of

* John 13:23, 19:26, 20:2, 21:7, 21:20.

holiness was appointed the Son of God in power by his resurrection from the dead: Jesus Christ our Lord. Through him we received grace and apostleship to call all the Gentiles to the obedience that comes from faith for his name's sake. And you also are among those Gentiles who are called to belong to Jesus Christ.

ROMANS 1:1-6

He could have easily stopped after 'Paul, a servant of Christ Jesus', but he gets distracted by the one he serves, Jesus, the Messiah, the Son of God, a descendent of David, who was resurrected from the dead, our Lord. For Paul it appears that the identity of Jesus is much more significant than his own identity.

This makes sense when we remember Paul's own story. Paul once had had a clear sense of his own identity and the identity of the Jewish people, so when this Christian movement started up within Judaism it shook him, and he found himself wanting to destroy these Christians before it could get established. But Jesus met him dramatically on the road to Damascus and Paul found himself asking, 'Who are you, Lord?' And Jesus replies, 'I am Jesus.' Paul's life was transformed by a revelation of who Jesus was and is. And when he understood who Jesus was, he began to understand his own identity.*

And who is this Jesus? Among many other things, he is the one who is loved by his Father. When Jesus first appears in public it is for his baptism, and he hears a voice from heaven saying, 'You are my son, whom I love, and with you I am very pleased.'** At this point in his life he has not done any miracles, or cast out any demons, or raised anyone from the dead. He has not taught anyone, or gathered a community of disciples, or challenged the authorities. He has not yet died for the sins of the world, conquering sin and suffering and death. He has done nothing worth recording in the Bible (other

* Acts 9.
** Mark 1:11.

than being born, and then running away from his parents briefly when he was twelve) and yet his Father loves him and is pleased with him. He has known this love from eternity, and he starts his public life totally secure in his identity as the beloved son of the Father.

We may not have known this love from eternity, but to be a Christian is to be one who is brought into this relationship with the Father who loves us. And so, for you too, before you have done anything, achieved anything, tried or failed at anything, you are loved by God. If everything else were stripped away from your life, this would remain: you are loved by God.

This was the starting point for Jesus' ministry. This is the starting point for Paul's letter to the Church in Rome. This is our starting point too. You are loved by God. This is your identity.

Elsewhere in the Bible, in 1 John 4:8, we read that 'God is love'. God is love: that is his identity. And you are loved: that is yours.

But if the love of God is your identity, then we need to understand what this love actually *is*. We need to understand the nature of the love of God.

PART ONE

The Nature of the Love of God
ROMANS 1–4

Chapter 2

POWER

For I am not ashamed of the gospel, because it is the power of God that brings salvation to everyone who believes: first to the Jew, then to the Gentile.

ROMANS 1:16

'We must discover the power of love, the power, the redemptive power of love. And when we discover that, we will be able to make this old world a new world. We will be able to make men better. Love is the only way.'*

MARTIN LUTHER KING

In this first part of Romans we see three characteristics of God's love: Power, Passion and Grace. We will take a chapter to look at each of them.

The first quality of God's love is power. God is all-powerful and he is all-loving. His power is always loving, and his love is always powerful. And this means that God's love is the answer to our weakness.

In 2020, after ten years working at St Peter's, Brighton, I was allowed a sabbatical, so Tara and I and our four children went to stay with St Stephen's Society in Hong Kong. This was an organization that I had been to visit four times previously, and which totally transformed my understanding of the power of God's love.

---

* Martin Luther King Jr., 'Loving Your Enemies', sermon delivered at Dexter Avenue Baptist Church, Montgomery, Alabama, November 1957.

It was started in 1966 when Jackie Pullinger, a twenty-one-year-old English woman, left England to become a missionary. She got on a boat that was sailing round the world and prayed that God would tell her when to get off. She got off in Hong Kong, with no money, no contacts and no plans, other than to tell people about Jesus. She soon found herself going into Kowloon Walled City, an area that had been excluded from the treaty between China and the UK, and consequently had become a haven for everything illegal or unpleasant, from gambling, drugs, prostitution to dentistry and dog restaurants. The housing blocks were so closely packed together that there was very little natural light. The Chinese simply called it 'Darkness'. The triads ruled it, the police rarely went in, and Westerners avoided it, but Jackie went in and started to get to know the inhabitants.

Her message was very simple: 'Jesus loves you.' And yet that simple message was also very powerful and what has happened as a result is told in her book, *Chasing the Dragon*. Heroin addicts came off drugs without pain by the power of the Holy Spirit, triad members became followers of Jesus, and this has continued for over fifty years. This is a place where it seems clearer than ever that God's love can change everything. It changes the lives of those who hear this message. And it has the power to change communities. The Walled City has been knocked down and replaced with a park, and in the middle is a rock with a plaque dedicated to Jackie.

Back in 2001 when I was helping in one of the houses there was a 'new boy' who came to live in the house. He had become a Christian through one of the outreach teams, and like everyone else, after two weeks of detoxing would stay for a year to grow in his faith and begin to find healing from everything that he had experienced before coming to faith. We quickly became good friends even though he spoke no English and I spoke no Cantonese. After I left, we kept in touch a little, but then didn't hear anything for a while. I visited again in 2006 and hoped my friend was still doing well, knowing that a relapse can be common. I was asking around to see if anyone knew him or remembered him, but people seemed to be busy getting ready for a wedding that was happening a few days later. Apparently two of the helpers were getting married and there were big celebrations planned. Eventually I found someone who knew my old friend, and they told me that he was doing well. He had completed the year, become a helper, had gone on mission trips to Thailand. Then they told me that it was his wedding they were planning for. Someone ran off to find him, and then suddenly there he was, talking to me in his much-improved English, and introducing me to his fiancée. I was thrilled to see him so well and happy, but also devastated to have to leave before the wedding.

Now fourteen years later I was keen to find out the rest of his story and see how he had been getting on. So when we arrived back in Sing Mun Springs I was overjoyed to find that he was living there too. He now had two boys, similar in age to our children, and after years of leading some of the houses here, was now running his own business. They had also opened up their home to two of the teenage girls who were part of St Stephen's. The love of God, which had transformed his life, was now being passed on.

What is it that makes the love of God so powerful?

THE POWERFUL LOVE OF GOD

Certainly, God has powerful emotions towards us. The Bible describes God's compassion for us, his delight over us, his longing for us. Our feelings of love tend to be some of the most powerful feelings we have, but they are a pale reflection of the powerful feelings of love that God has towards you. No one has ever felt as strongly about you than God has in his love. But the power of God's love is more than his feelings.

God's words of love are powerful. Our words have power to hurt or encourage, affirm or abuse, lie or tell the truth. But God's words have the power to create the world, life, miracles. Whatever words have been spoken over your life which have hurt you or discouraged you or confused you, know that God's words over you are words of love, and are far more powerful than any of the words human beings can say to you. But the power of God's love is more than his words.

God's love is so powerful because it has been expressed supremely in an event: the death and resurrection of Jesus Christ. This is the 'Gospel' which Paul refers to in Romans 1:16. The Gospel is the great story of God's love for us, which culminates with Jesus, the embodiment of love. This story has changed reality forever, for on the cross Jesus took on himself everything that is wrong with each of us, and with the world, and defeated them. Everything that gets in the way of love, undermining it or diluting it, or separating us from it, was destroyed. On the cross God defeated all that opposes and frustrates and separates us from love.

And then he poured out his own Spirit, his own love into our hearts. The Spirit is the power, God's loving power and powerful love, who is within each of us when we believe in Jesus.

That is why God's love is so powerful. And that is why you never need to feel powerless. You are not weak, because you are loved by God.

Paul writes that the Gospel – the story of God's love for us – is the power of God for *salvation* (1:16). 'Salvation' refers to 'the total putting right of all things'. In other words, there is no part of your life that God's love cannot transform. It reaches into the deepest parts of your life, and into every part of your life. And it is for *everyone who believes*. No one is excluded from the power of this love. No one needs to feel powerless.

OUR WEAKNESS

One of the worst aspects of chronic fatigue is the endless feeling of weakness: physically, mentally and emotionally. I suppose that we must all feel weak at some point, feeling powerless over our circumstances, our relationships or over our own impulses and desires. We can feel powerless to change ourselves; we can feel powerless to make a difference in the world.

After declaring the power of God for salvation in 1:16, Paul goes on to describe all kinds of problems he sees with humanity. These are areas of our lives where we might feel weak or powerless to change, but God's love is the power of salvation for every aspect of our lives.

God's love is more powerful than the problems in your *mind*. Paul writes about their 'futile' thinking (1:21). We do not value what we should value, and we do value what we shouldn't value. We don't see ourselves as we really are. It's like we're all looking at ourselves in the curved mirrors one finds at the funfair. In these mirrors there are some parts that appear bigger than they really are, and some parts of us much smaller. We do not see the world as it really is. We tend to embrace fantasy over reality. But the love of God is more powerful than our false thinking. It is stronger than the lies we tell ourselves. It is a love that brings about the renewal of our minds and enables us to see ourselves, other people and the world more truthfully. For in his death Jesus was condemned based on false accusations and so on the cross Jesus took on himself all falsehood and confusion, exchanging these things for truth.

God's love is more powerful than the problems in your *heart*. Next Paul says that 'their foolish hearts were darkened' (1:21). We all struggle to some degree with insecurity, fear, jealousy, and a lack of compassion. But God's love is more powerful than all our emotional struggles, changing the way that we react to the situations we face, transforming the way that we feel about other people and the way we feel about ourselves. For on the cross Jesus' heart was broken, he cried out in distress, and absorbed into himself all emotional pain, giving us instead peace and joy.

God's love is more powerful than the problems with your *desires*. We desire things that are not good for us, and we don't desire things that are good for us. Paul writes about our sexuality (1:24–28) as something broken. Our sexuality is a good part of us, also created by God. But like our minds and our hearts, all sexual desire is to some degree broken and imperfect, and in need of healing and transformation. And the love of God is stronger than the struggles we have with sex and sexuality and has the potential to redirect our desires to what is good and right. For Jesus took on our broken sexuality on the cross. He was stripped naked, taking on our shame and making us pure.

God's love is more powerful than the problems with your *relationships*. Paul was writing to a community with deep divisions between the Gentile Christians and Jewish Christians, where the relationship between these groups was characterized by hostility, mistrust, and competition. All our relationships are broken to some degree. We are all dysfunctional in the way we relate to one another. And the world in general is full of so much hatred, loneliness and division. And yet the love of God is stronger than the problems in our relationships, bringing reconciliation, belonging and unity. For Jesus himself was betrayed, abandoned, mocked and abused on the cross, and in experiencing these things took into himself all our relational pain to defeat it forever, and to give us the possibility of unity, reconciliation and intimacy.

There is no part of your life that God's love cannot touch and restore. God's love caused Jesus to take on himself all that is wrong, in order to give you all that is right. That is the reason that God's love has the power to transform every part of who you are: our minds, our hearts, and our desires; and every aspect of what you do: your relationships, your work and your rest.

THE DEEP PLACES

The love of God touches and transforms the deep places within us, the roots of our pain and our dysfunctions. Paul is not only describing physical, emotional or mental problems, but also spiritual ones. Our minds don't understand God as he really is, our hearts are not aligned to him, we do not desire him as we should, but also even deeper than these is the problem of love: our experience of being unloved, and our inability to love others.

The fundamental problem with the world is not political, or philosophical, or biological, but spiritual. We were made for God but find ourselves separated from him. That is why the love of God is the answer to our weakness, because only this can meet our deepest needs and fulfil our greatest longings.

The most broken parts of us are broken because of a lack of love – when we haven't been loved or when we have failed to love others. The deepest wounds come either where we haven't been loved as we should have been or when we have failed to love those we were meant to love. It is the lack of love that is at the root of all our dysfunctions. So it is only love that has the power to put us back together. The love of God is the only thing powerful enough to touch and heal the very deepest parts of your life, mending those wounds, supplying what was lacking, putting right what once went wrong.

SOLUTIONS AND PROBLEMS

In this opening section of Romans Paul starts by stating the solution (the Gospel which is powerful for salvation for everyone who believes) and only then moves on to talk about all the problems. All the painful complexities of our broken lives, all our failures to live as we should live, described over almost three chapters, but he has already told us that there is a solution to everything and for everyone. They are problems for which he has already declared there is a solution.

I have four children, and I have no idea what challenges and difficulties they are going to face in their lives. I know that I cannot protect them from what is ahead, nor should I try to shield them from every disappointment and heartache, or from making their own mistakes, but what I can do is try to pour into them as much love and encouragement, wisdom and confidence, character and faith as I can, so that when painful times come and they feel rejected, or when they make mistakes and feel ashamed, they will have the tools to deal with them. I am trying to instill in them the solutions before they face the problems.

The love of God is the solution that precedes the problem. You can go through life already possessing the solution, knowing that whatever challenges and problems come your way you already possess the answer, which is the love of God. The Bible speaks of a God who saves us in the midst of distress and trouble. God doesn't promise us an easy life, but he promises to love us with a love that is powerful.

EMPOWERED AND POWERLESS

This love is empowering, but it also enables us to embrace our powerlessness. We no longer need to control everything or everyone, dominate or manipulate, for there is a love that sets us free to be weak, to rest in the arms of the Almighty who loves us.

Paul was writing to a community in Rome, which was the centre of power in the most powerful empire the world had ever seen. The Christians living there would have been surrounded by symbols of power like the Roman Forum, the temple of Julius Caesar, and other symbols of economic, military and technological power. But for Paul there was a symbol of much greater power, even though it looked like a symbol of powerlessness. On the face of it the cross looks like powerlessness because it is a symbol of rejection and apparent failure, but in reality it is a symbol of the greatest act of love in the history of the world. What was a symbol of powerlessness has become for us a symbol of power.

You might feel weak and powerless over your circumstances or over temptations, unable to change the situation you find yourself in or to make a difference in the world, but you have this symbol of the cross, this sign that God's love might look powerless, but is really the most powerful thing in the world. It is the skeleton key that opens every lock. It reaches deeper than we could ever imagine. It reaches wider, touching every area of your life. And it can give you confidence that no matter what you face, or what difficulties come your way, you have the most powerful force in the world in your life.

Chapter 3

PASSION

The wrath of God is being revealed from heaven against all the godlessness and wickedness of people, who suppress the truth by their wickedness.

ROMANS 1:18

'The wrath of God is the love of God.'*

EMIL BRUNNER

'Isn't she marvellous when she's angry?'**

PHYLLIS WATERBURY

God's love is powerful, but it is also passionate. It is not an impersonal force. Nor it is a theoretical principle. The Bible speaks of a love that is personal and emotive. And so, within the first chapter of Romans we encounter talk of God's anger, or 'wrath'.

For many people (including me) there is something uncomfortable about the concept of God's anger. I am aware that my natural tendency is to try to avoid my own anger or other people's anger directed towards me. I hated being told off as a child, and still don't cope very well with people who are cross with me. I'm not very good with conflict and generally want everyone to get on. Consequently, I've tended to avoid thinking about God's anger, skipping over those parts of the Bible which speak of it, and trying instead to

---

* Emil Brunner, *Man in Revolt*, The Lutterworth Press, 2003, p187.
** *The Railway Children*, directed by Lionel Jeffries, EMI Elstree, 1970.

focus on the love of God, which I preferred to understand more in terms of his patience, kindness, comfort and affirmation.

However, the more I have thought about God's love the more I have been forced to think about God's anger. And I have realized that anger is an essential part of love, and that if God is loving then it is vital that God is also angry. For if God loves us, he must care about our lives. It must matter to him what happens to us, and what we choose to do. And if God cares then we cannot escape that God will be angry. For anger is the recognition that something is not right and needs to change.

I can now see that my own anger is often linked to love. I get angry with my children, not despite loving them, but because I love them. I get angry about things that aren't right in the world, not because I hate the world, but because I love the world. God's anger is an essential part of his love, because it shows that he cares about us – what we do and what happens to us.

Human anger, though often justified in some way, is also mixed with violence, hatred, harsh words and being out of control. However, God's anger is not like ours. Whereas our anger is often irrational, and chaotic, God is repeatedly described in the Bible as 'slow to anger and abounding in love'.*

At the time Paul was writing the two main philosophical schools were the Epicureans and the Stoics. For the Epicureans the highest virtue was *ataraxia* – a life without trouble – which meant trying to avoid anything painful or difficult. For the Stoics, however, the highest ideal was *apatheia* (from which we get the word apathy or apathetic), which meant not being affected by suffering. The choice was therefore between avoiding suffering or trying to remain unaffected by it. However, the Christian response to suffering should be neither avoidance nor apathy, but love. For love is not removed from pain or difficulty but is intimately engaged with it.

* See Psalm 86:15, Psalm 103:8.

When Paul writes about the anger (or wrath) of God in Romans 18, he refers to two objects of God's anger: 'godlessness' and 'wickedness'.

ANGER AND INJUSTICE

The word translated often as 'wickedness' literally means 'injustice'. The love of God compels him to respond to injustice with anger. His love is a love that confronts injustice.

In April 1994 there was an outbreak of extreme violence in Rwanda, leading to a period of one hundred days in which 800,000 Rwandans were killed. Women and children were hacked to death, many of them hiding in churches which they had hoped would be places of refuge. It constituted some of the most appalling violence since the Second World War. As part of the response to the genocide, the U.N. sent an American civil rights lawyer who had been working for the US Department of Justice, Gary Haugen. His task was to lead the investigations and work out how this had happened. Gary Haugen was deeply affected by what he saw there, and as a result set up the organization International Justice Mission, which seeks to promote justice around the world.

In his book, *Good News about Injustice*, Haugen writes about the anger of God,

> The knowledge of God's great anger toward and condemnation of injustice is what gives me hope to seek justice in this world. Standing with my boots deep in the reeking muck of a Rwandan mass grave, where thousands of innocent people have been horribly slaughtered, I have no words, no meaning, no life, no hope, if there is not a God of history and time who is absolutely outraged, absolutely furious, absolutely burning with anger toward those who took it into their own hands to commit such acts.[*]

* Gary Haugen, *Good News about Injustice*, IVP, 2009, p100.

It is essential to God's nature as one who loves us that he is angry when he sees suffering and injustice in our world. For if he were not angry, it would mean he didn't care. And if he didn't care, then he would not be loving.

God's love requires that he care about the great injustices we see in the world: poverty, racism, inequality, slavery, abuse. But it also means that God cares about each of the individual injustices that we experience. Everything in our lives which is unjust, or unfair, whether caused by abuse, neglect, or ignorance, God sees and it breaks his heart. Those things that hurt us deeply and that feel so unfair, hurt God deeply and that makes him angry.

God cares about the things that happen to us because he loves us. But God also cares about the things that we *do* in our life, the choices we make for ourselves, because he loves us.

After I left university, I worked for a while as a nanny (or 'manny'), mainly looking after a twelve-year-old boy called Tom, who had suffered a huge amount of neglect in his life. His mother was struggling with heroin addiction and couldn't look after him, and he didn't know who his father was. He was put into the care of his uncle who was struggling to manage him, and who hired me to look after him.

When I first met Tom, he told me that he wanted to be evil, and there were some real challenges with his behaviour. As I got to know him, I realized that he owned some violent and inappropriate video games which were rated 18 and as I didn't think that they were helping his behaviour, I decided to confiscate them. He told me that I was being unfair and got quite angry with me, but I held my ground.

Over that period of looking after him I realized just how desperate he was to be loved. He would take my hand and look up at me and say, 'Jonny, do you love me?' After about eighteen months he went to boarding school and I stopped working for his uncle, but in the holidays, I sometimes got to see him. On one of those occasions, he took me up to his bedroom, and I saw another violent, 18-rated, game on his bed. It had seemed that he wanted me to notice it, but then made a show of wanting to hide it, and he started pleading with me not to take it away. I was a bit confused and told him that I didn't work for his uncle anymore, so I couldn't take it away or tell him what to do. However, rather than being relieved, he seemed disappointed, and looked up at me with these big, brown eyes, and said, 'You can take them away if you want … I want you to take them away.'

Then I understood what was going on. He wanted me to be cross with him. More than anything that boy wanted someone to care about the actions he took, because caring about what he did meant that they loved him.

God cares passionately about the choices you make in your life, and he cares passionately when you hurt other people or yourself. And he wants the best for you. Paul writes a little later, 'all have sinned and fall short of the glory of God' (3:23). When you love someone, you want the best for them. We were made for glorious lives, but we fall short.

There are three kinds of feedback that we can receive from people when we've done something wrong or are not doing what we should be doing. We can be told that everything is fine when it is not, or that it doesn't matter when it does. This is the denial of reality and doesn't help anyone. The second type of response is to write us off as a result of our failings, telling us that we are useless or terrible people, and there's nothing that can be done. But the third type of feedback is where someone confronts what is wrong in us, while providing us with a solution.

This is how God relates to us and to the things that are not right in our lives. He does not ignore them or suggest they don't matter, nor does he give up on us as a result. He confronts what is not right, showing us that the things in our lives are far worse than we might like to pretend, and yet at the same time providing the solution.

ANGER AND REJECTION

The anger of God is also directed against 'godlessness'. This refers to the rejection of God. We may feel like we don't want God to care whether we believe in him or not, but to ask God to be indifferent to how we respond to him is really to ask him not to love us at all.

The more you love someone, the more you invest in that person, and the more you open yourself to being hurt by that person. God loves us completely, he invests in us completely, and so when we reject him, or ignore him, it affects him. The God who loves us so much is not indifferent to our response to him. He would not be a truly loving God if he didn't care either way.

If on the day that I proposed to Tara I'd said to her, 'Will you marry me? However, just so you know, it doesn't matter to me if it's a yes or a no. I really don't care either way.' But that would not be a statement of love, but of indifference.

We might say that had I been rejected I would have been *hurt* rather than angry. However, hurt and anger are closely connected. Hurt is anger turned inwards; anger is hurt turned outwards. And God is hurt by our rejection of him. He allows himself to have his heart broken. But he is also angry. This is vital. For anger, at its best, can be a powerful driving force in our lives. It can cause terrible damage if misdirected or out of control, but it can also motivate us to do great things for good. I know people whose anger at injustice has caused them to travel great distances, make huge sacrifices and do extraordinary things. Anger has caused people to fight racism and the destruction of the planet, to stand up to bullies, start campaigns, and expose illegal and immoral activities. And God's anger is a powerful driving force for good. The Old Testament prophet Jeremiah wrote, 'The anger of the LORD will not turn back until he has accomplished everything that he has put in his heart to do.'*

* Jeremiah 23:20.

Anger was a driving force in the life of Jesus. Jesus was so angry at the corruption in the temple that he got a whip and drove out all the sellers and animals. He was so angry at the grave of Lazarus that he raised him from the dead. Jesus was so angry at all the sin and suffering and death in the world that he went to the cross in order to end them forever. The anger of God points us to a God who cares about the state of the world and is driven by that anger to put things right.

As a child I shared a room with my older brother and younger sister, and quite often, after we had been tucked up in bed, we would get out of bed and start playing games. We thought our parents had no idea what we were doing, not realizing how thin the ceiling was. Our parents would be in the sitting room, listening to the sound of us crashing around, and eventually decide to do something about it, and they would come up and tell us off. Although I didn't like being told off, it strikes me now that their anger brought them physically closer: from the sitting room downstairs into the bedroom close to us.

God's anger is the same. God's anger brings him closer. God's anger brought him from heaven to earth to deal once and for all with everything that is wrong with the world. He did not do this by taking his anger out on humanity, but by absorbing the anger into himself on the cross. All injustice and godlessness and their consequences were taken up into himself to be defeated once and for all. And God continues to act to put right what has gone wrong in our lives, whether the wrongs we have done or the wrongs done to us. God's passionate involvement in our lives defeats and transforms all that is not right in them. Because he loves us.

Chapter 4

GRACE

… and all are justified freely by his grace through the redemption that came by Christ Jesus.

ROMANS 3:24

'If Cinderella says, "How is it that I must leave the ball at twelve?" her godmother might answer, "How is it that you are going there till twelve?"'*

G.K. CHESTERTON

God's love is powerful, in that it has the power to change everything in our lives – the way we think, feel, act, and love other people. God's love is passionate, for he cares about us – what we do and what happens to us. And now we see a third aspect of God's love for us: Grace. God's love is gracious, for it is freely given to us.

In Romans 3:21–31, having spent much of the preceding section writing about the problems with humanity, Paul now describes what God has done to put it all right.

First, he summarizes the problem: 'All have sinned and fall short of the glory of God.' He refers to something in the past ('all *have* sinned') and something in the present ('*fall short*'), for all of us have things that we've done that we regret, or wished had happened differently, and all of us have struggles in the present, where we fail to live as we might want. There are aspects of all our lives which aren't right: things that hurt God, hurt other people, and hurt ourselves. The problem is not just with a certain group of people, but with everyone. The problem is not with one element of our lives, but with every part of our lives. It is not a surface level

* G. K. Chesterton, *Orthodoxy,* Hodder and Stoughton, 1999, pp76–77.

problem, but one that affects our very core. It is a universal problem affecting every part of every person.

Second, he announces the solution: 'all are justified'. To be 'justified' means to be declared innocent, put right, liberated from our sin. So, Paul is saying that all your sins, past, present and future, have been dealt with and you are in the clear. You are not only forgiven; you have also been given a new status. It is the opposite of condemnation. You are permanently accepted and approved of. Now, all obstacles in your relationship with God have been removed and nothing can separate you from God's love.

And all of this has been achieved through the grace of God. For we are justified freely *by his grace*.

Once, when our children were young, I was making flapjacks while everyone else was having breakfast in our kitchen. Having cooked the flapjacks in the oven, I was trying to dig them out of the baking tray with a small, sharp knife. As I did this I slipped and the knife cut into my other hand, just below the thumb. And I knew immediately that it had gone very deep and that this was a serious injury.

I'm not very good with blood or cuts, and have a tendency to overreact, but in this case, I knew that I had done myself some serious damage and might lose my thumb at the very least, if not my life if, as I suspected, I had hit an artery.

As panic set in, I went to the sink to run it under cold water (I'm not sure why I thought this was a good idea, I'd possibly got confused with burns) and Tara rushed over to see what was happening. She asked to see the cut, but I warned her it was *really* bad. She examined the wound and then told me firmly, but calmly, 'Jonny, there is almost no blood.'

But it was not enough to settle me. I started to feel light-headed, the room began to spin, and I passed out on the floor.

When I regained consciousness, I was aware that Tara was directing the operations to keep me alive/help Daddy with the tiny cut on his hand. One of the children was holding a wound dressing against the cut on my hand. In my mind he was holding it against the cut to stop me bleeding to death, though in hindsight he was really just holding my hand. Another child had got me a pillow for my head. A third child was giving me hugs. Then the child who had got me a pillow started bouncing a ball next to my head. And our fourth child was continuing to eat her cornflakes, oblivious to what was taking place.

This is a small (and inadequate) picture of grace. I was experiencing the undeserved kindness of my family, when I was weak, helpless and unable to help myself. It was undeserved, for I had actually managed to upset Tara that very morning by somehow giving the impression to her that I was more interested in watching the highlights of a football game than I was in listening to her.

Nor was it something I could ever repay. Two days later, Tara cut herself while peeling an orange for the children. She cried out in pain, telling me what she had done. I thought to myself, 'Tara was so kind to me when I'd cut myself; I really want to do the same ... ' And I ended up doing exactly the same – I lay down on the floor feeling faint, and the children had to come and look after me again.

Grace is God's undeserved kindness to us. It is the freely given goodness of God poured into our lives. It is *undeserved*: for it is not a right or something to which we are entitled. It is actually the opposite of what we deserve.

It is *free*. It is not a reward. It is not earned. It is not a salary. It is a free gift.

It is *personal*. What we are given freely is Jesus Christ himself. As Paul writes in another of his letters, 'The son of God who loved me and gave *himself* for me.'*

And it is *total*. Grace comes to us through Jesus' death on the cross ('through the redemption which came through Jesus Christ'). It is free for us, but not for Jesus, for it is only through his death on

---

* Galatians 2:20.

the cross where he absorbed all our shame, guilt, and pride into himself and destroyed them once and for all. Jesus Christ gave himself totally for us, giving his life and his death. He sacrificed everything in order to give us everything. It is total grace.

This is the love of God. Grace is how God loves us. It defines how God relates to human beings.

And as we will see in the next chapter, it is received by *faith*. Grace is love given; faith is love received. Faith is trusting that this love is real and taking hold of what is freely given.

This has a number of consequences for us.

PROVING

This gracious love of God removes the need to try to prove yourself. The world around us might always be trying to convince you that you have to prove that you are loveable, but the grace of God means that you are already loved.

You do not need to defend yourself, or justify yourself, or explain yourself, because God's love comes to us 'apart from the law' (3:21). This means that it is not earned by our efforts.

If there is any question whether we are doing the right thing, or have done the right thing in the past, it is natural to try to justify ourselves. If I have been criticized, I want to explain myself. If I have got something wrong, I want people to think that I actually got it right. But the love of God removes any need to defend or explain or justify ourselves, for he justifies us freely and totally.

You do not need to prove yourself. You do not need to explain yourself. You do not need to justify yourself. You can live confidently in God's love for you.

There was a time at St Peter's when we had some work being done on the male toilets, and so one of the sets of female toilets was briefly used as the male toilets. However, the signs weren't very clear, and force of habit meant that women in the church would often use these toilets unaware that there had been a change. One day I went to these toilets (that had been the ladies' but were now the men's) when no one else was in there. I went into a cubicle, but when, after some time, I came out, the room was full of women. They were all looking at me thinking, 'What is the associate vicar doing in the ladies' toilets?' Everything in me wanted to explain and justify myself, to show them that I was in the right and they were wrong. But then I remembered this passage, that God had justified me and there was no need to justify myself to anyone. So I just said, 'Morning everyone,' and walked out!

COMPETING

God's gracious love also means that there is no need to compare yourself or compete against other people. For there is an abundance of this grace.

Before I was married I went on holiday with around twenty friends to France. One of the people I went with was working for a manufacturer of high-quality chocolate, and she brought with her enough chocolate that all of us could eat as much as we wanted all week without us ever running out. During that week's holiday at no point did anyone look around them and complain about how much chocolate someone else was eating, because there was an abundance of chocolate.

In contrast, occasionally I'll pop down the shops to fetch a small bar of chocolate to share with Tara. These are normally divided into six sections, and we are always very aware of how much chocolate the other person has had, because there is a scarcity of chocolate.

Living in God's love is like living in a holiday chalet in France surrounded by chocolate that will never run out. There is not a scarcity of love, but an abundance of love. There is no limit to God's forgiveness, blessing, kindness and grace in Jesus Christ. I know that when I start comparing myself with other people, or competing for approval or position, it is because I have started living as though there were a scarcity of God's love, rather than an abundance.

This means that the love of God has the ability to overcome our differences and our hostility to one another. When Paul writes, 'there is no difference … all have sinned and fall short of the glory of God' (3:22–23), he is referring to the difference between Jews and Gentiles. In the ancient world there was no greater difference than the difference between Jew and Gentile. Jews would not even eat with Gentiles. Each group thought that they were better than the other group. The Jewish Christians thought that the Gentiles were immoral. The Gentile Christians thought that the Jewish Christians were self-righteous and restrictive. But Paul insists that each group is equally 'sinful' and equally 'justified', and there is enough grace for everyone.

There is no need to compare or compete. Everyone has sinned. Everyone is justified. And God's grace is available for all.

PRETENDING

God's grace is what enables us to connect to our brokenness. Paul's statement that 'all have sinned and fall short of the glory of God' is not something that he would have always believed. For much of his life he would have seen 'sinners' as referring to other people, who were not able to live up to the standards that he had for his own life. But when he encountered Jesus Christ and experienced his grace, it enabled him to own his mistakes and struggles. He was no longer afraid of his own weaknesses or failings. He writes honestly about his struggles in Romans and elsewhere because he knows that he is loved.

God's grace makes it safe to recognize our brokenness, for neither our past mistakes nor our present struggles are obstacles to God loving us. The classic hymn, *Amazing Grace* begins, 'Amazing grace, how sweet the sound, that saved a wretch like me.' The amazing grace of God enables us to see our own wretchedness, for we are loved even in the brokenness. And the more amazing the grace of God becomes to us, the more we are able to see our wretchedness.

God's gracious love means that you do not need to pretend you're better than you are. Nor do you need to despair when you've messed up. Sometimes it can be tempting to think, 'I've really messed up, I don't know how I can get back on track after I've done this'. And when I feel that I sense God saying to me, 'Do you really think that what you've done is bigger than my love? Do you really think you could do anything that could defeat my love for you?'

This is true for us, and it is true for other people. When we refuse to forgive other people for what they have done, it is like we are saying that God's love is not able to overcome this thing, that his grace is too small to bring about restoration or reconciliation.

THE LENS OF GRACE

This gracious love has the potential to change the way that we see the world. We can see the world through different lenses. We can see the world through the victim lens (aware of all the ways that we have been wronged), through the lens of lack (focussing on everything we have been, or are currently, missing out on), through the lens of entitlement (we have a right to everything), or we can see the world through the lens of grace, in which we see everything as a gift.

When I left school one of the first books I read was *Orthodoxy* by G.K. Chesterton, and it changed my life. In it he insists that we should see the world as if it were a fairy tale. For in a fairy tale, the characters tend not complain about the way that the world works. When the fairy godmother appears to Cinderella and announces that her rags will turn into a beautiful dress, a pumpkin will become a coach, the mice horses to pull it, and that she 'shall go to the ball', she adds that it will only last until midnight. At this point Cinderella does not start complaining that it won't last till 2am, or ask why it couldn't be extended till the early afternoon on the following day, for the obvious reply would be, 'Why do you get to have any of it for any time?' For it is all a gift. It is all grace.

The whole world is a gift, freely and graciously given to us by God. It does not exist by necessity or as a reward. It is simply a gift.

Paul seems to see everything through the lens of grace. He sees his identity in terms of the grace of God, for he says, 'By the grace of God I am what I am.' He sees marital status through the lens of grace, for he describes both marriage and singleness as 'gifts'. He even connects his calling as an apostle to grace. This is extraordinary considering this calling meant being rejected by his own people, arrested, imprisoned, stoned, shipwrecked, beaten and whipped. Even the most painful experience in his life, his 'thorn' mentioned in 2 Corinthians (referring to some kind of torment that he experienced and which he pleaded with God to remove) is seen in the light of God's grace, for in the midst of this suffering he writes that God spoke to him, saying, 'My grace is sufficient for you, and my power is made perfect in weakness.'*

THE LIFE OF THE BELOVED

The gracious love of God changes the way we see the world. And it changes the ways we act towards the world. God's grace to us enables us to live gracious lives. In his book, *Life of the Beloved*, Henri Nouwen describes living in the love of God as being 'taken, blessed, broken and given.'** We are taken, for God takes hold of us, rescues us, and makes us his own. We are blessed, for God pours good things into our lives – his affirmation, provision, inspiration, guidance and transformation. Then we are broken, for inevitably we will go through times when things fall apart, when life makes no sense, our hearts are broken and our spirits are crushed. But finally

---

* 1 Corinthians 15:10, 1 Corinthians 7:7, 15:15–16, 2 Corinthians 12:9.
** Henri Nouwen, *Life of the Beloved*, John Murray Press, 2016.

we are given, for out of the blessings and the brokenness we are able to give our lives to others. The blessings are given and the brokenness is given. Our lives become channels of God's grace.

'BUT NOW'

The gracious love of God means that we now live in a whole new situation. Romans 3:21–31 begins with the words 'but now'. Martin Lloyd-Jones writes, 'There are no more wonderful words in the whole of Scripture than these two words: "But now".'* They insist that something has happened, a fundamental change has taken place, and a new relationship has been made possible. The gracious love of God has created a whole new situation, a whole new reality for each of us.

Raniero Cantalamessa, the Preacher to the Papal Household, uses this image to describe Paul's experience of grace.** Imagine someone walking through a dark forest in the middle of the night, holding just a small candle. The light of the candle is the light of our own efforts, our own comparing and competing, the light of our attempts to justify ourselves and to prove our worth in the world. And we are surrounded by fears and anxieties in this forest. But then the dawn comes, and the light of day which floods into the forest is so much bigger and greater and stronger than anything that we've experienced before. Suddenly we don't need the small candle anymore; we can throw it away. Instead we can live in the light of God's gracious love for us.

God's love is powerful, passionate and gracious. And because it is gracious it is like a gift. And because it is a gift, it needs to be received. Which leads us to the next theme: faith.

---

* Martyn Lloyd-Jones, *Romans: An Exposition of Chapters 3:20–4:25, Atonement and Justification*, 1998, p25.
** Raniero Cantalamessa, *Life in Christ*, Liturgical Press, 1990, p41.

PART TWO

Responding to the Love of God (1)
ROMANS 3

Chapter 5

RECEIVING GOD'S LOVE

'This righteousness is given from God through faith in Jesus
Christ to all who believe.'
ROMANS 3:22

'This is faith: that I let Jesus Christ be for me what I am
not and cannot be for myself: my truth, my goodness, my
righteousness, my salvation; that I let the Word of God be
my God, my Creator and Preserver, my Lord and Saviour.'*

KARL BARTH

What are you supposed to do with this love that God has for you?
How are you supposed to respond?

Our first response is faith. For Paul insists that this love is received
by faith, which means that you start by letting God love you.

After being ill for about six months, I went to see the same wise
monk who had spoken those challenging and life-changing words
to me when I'd first got ill. At that time he was living in a monastery
in the south of France. I thought I would go for a couple of weeks,
and knowing it was a (mostly) silent monastery, I packed a bag full
of books and set off. He collected me from the airport, driving me
to the monastery in a very old car, which he drove very fast and
with apparent full confidence in the resurrection. When we got to
the monastery he took me to my room, sat down, paused, smiled
and then said to me, 'Jonny, you don't let people love you. Why is
this?' I had been expecting more questions on how my journey had

---

* Karl Barth, *God Here and Now*, Routledge, 2003, p26.

been, or what I'd been up to recently, so I was a little taken aback. I responded that I thought people did love me. I felt very grateful that I was loved. But he replied, 'Yes, but you don't let people love you.'

This statement, as I allowed it to sink in over those two weeks and then in the months that followed, changed everything for me. I began to see the ways that I had been rejecting and refusing the love of those closest to me. I would often refuse offers of help or be uncomfortable people doing things for me unless I could pay them back. I realized that I had also been keeping God at a distance, refusing his help and resisting his love. From that point onwards, I began to try to let God love me, and to let other people love me.

God loves you, graciously, passionately and powerfully, but it is not imposed upon you. This love is unconditional, but God does not force you to receive it. You are free to refuse him. You are free to reject him. You might feel that you don't want this love, or need this love, or trust this love.

Or you can choose to receive this love. This is faith: the decision to open yourself up to this love which is freely given to you. At its simplest, faith is letting God love you. All our lives we have been refusing God, pushing him away, keeping him at a distance, saying 'no' to him, but faith is where we stop running and finally let him in. Faith is saying, 'Yes' to the God who loves us.

TRUSTING IN THE LOVE OF GOD

The Western world has normally valued independence and self-reliance. It is difficult to admit that we need anyone or anything. There is a kind of safety to be found in pushing people away, keeping everyone (including God) at a distance. But faith is where we let God in and begin to trust that this love for us is real.

Faith is more than believing God exists; it means also believing that God loves you. Right at the start of the Bible, Adam and Eve are given a garden to live in and enjoy. It was a gift, freely given to them. But there was one thing that was forbidden for them: to eat from the tree of the knowledge of good and evil. This is exactly what they did, and in doing so they acted without faith. In eating the fruit, Adam and Eve did not disbelieve the existence of God. At no point do they cease to believe that God created them, had spoken to them, or had given them this garden. But they did not trust him. More specifically, they did not trust that he loved them. They doubted that his command to them was for their own good, given to them because he loved them.

Faith is trusting in God's love for us. That's why Abraham is the supreme example of faith for Paul. God asks Abraham to trust him at three significant moments in his life. First, he asks him to leave his country and head off to a new land which God will only tell him about later. This meant leaving Ur, a big and important city, a cultural centre for the area, and go instead to somewhere not only unknown but also far less exciting. Then he asks him to trust him for a son, when both he and his wife are much too old to have children. Finally, having been given this son, God asks him to sacrifice this son to him, wanting to see if Abraham will trust him enough to give up the thing that he loves most in all the world. In each case, Abraham had to trust that God loved him to respond with faith. Abraham's faith was not just in the existence of God, but in the God who loved him.

FAITH AND REPENTANCE

Faith often means giving something up so that we can receive something greater, letting go of something we love to take hold of something even greater.

My sister and brother-in-law once gave us a particularly generous present for Christmas. They had a friend who was a farmer and they gave us two topside joints, a brisket, sirloin and rump steaks, braising steak, stewing steak and minced beef (essentially, they gave us half a cow to eat). Only they didn't actually give us the meat, but they gave us the promise of this meat. It was all paid for. All we had to do was call up the farm and arrange for it to be delivered.

However, we didn't have a big freezer, and what we had was already full of fishfingers and frozen peas and ice cream, so we didn't order it straight away. We had this wonderful present waiting for us, but we didn't have the space for it. And so it waited and waited. Eventually we realized we had to do something, and so we ate a lot of fishfingers and frozen peas to make space, ordered the meat and ate beef every day for the next month.

The love of God is like a beautiful gift that is waiting for us, but we can find that we haven't really received it. It's not that it's not wanted; it's just that we don't have the space in our lives for it right now. We are too filled up with other things.

In the Gospels' faith is often connected with repentance. Repentance is a change of mind, a change of heart, a change of how we live. It is letting go of one way of living so that we can embrace a new way. It is emptying out of what is not good, in order to be refilled with something better. When you repent, you are letting go of living without God's love. You are emptying out all your attempts to live independently of God's love. All so that you can make space for the greatest gift of all.

FAITH IN A PERSON

This faith is not trusting in something abstract; it is faith in a person. It is specific and personal. Christianity is not about faith in general, but faith in Jesus Christ in particular. It is not faith in a belief system, a way of life, a religion or a community; it is faith in a person. And it is certainly not faith in ourselves, or in humanity, but in one who is outside of ourselves, who alone can be relied on perfectly. Therefore, it is not the quantity of faith that counts, but the object of your faith.

I once had complete faith that I could do a handstand push-up. I got into a headstand position (with help from my children), and there was no doubt in my mind that I would be able to push the whole of my weight upwards. My faith in my own strength was total. Initially it felt like it was going to be too difficult, but then I started to believe. Something welled up within me and I knew I could do it. And then I began to push upwards like I hadn't done before.

Unfortunately, it made no difference. My head stayed on the floor. Because I can't actually do handstand push-ups, and no amount of faith was going to help me. There was no problem with the quantity of faith, just the object of my faith (which was myself). The best-selling song *I believe I can fly* is fine if taken metaphorically, or with the help of a flying machine or apparatus, or if it were to be sung by (most) birds. But no matter how much a human may believe he or she can fly, it won't help to make that a reality.

You need to put our faith in the right thing, or more precisely, in the right person. In the one who is the guarantee that you are loved, who is the embodiment of love, who has demonstrated once and for all that you are loved. Faith is putting yourself into the hands of Jesus – your past and future, your work and rest, what you do, who you love, where you live.

TOTAL TRUST

There is often a moment when you will have to make a leap, from one way of operating to another.

I once took my children on something that claimed to be a 'treetops adventure'. It involved each of us putting on a harness, connecting ourselves to a wire that would hold us if we fell, and then trying to walk across a series of terrifying bridges, from treetop to treetop. As we walked around, my children loving it while I did my best not to reveal my inner terror, I held on tightly to anything

I could, making sure my feet were as securely placed as possible. We were told that should we fall, the harness would hold us, but I certainly wasn't going to test this.

But then we got the end of the route, and on to a small platform, where someone attached us and our harnesses to a zip wire. All we had to do was jump off the platform and 'zip' happily to ground level. What was required at this point was a complete change in my approach. Up to this point I had been trusting in my own strength and ability, vaguely and inadequately comforted by an assurance that my harness would hold me if I fell. But I was doing everything I could to ensure that we wouldn't need to test this claim. But now, in order to get to where I needed to be, I had to jump off and trust the harness completely. This felt very unnatural, as I'd spent the whole of my life trying not to fall off tall structures, but I knew that this was the only way to get to where I wanted to be, and so I took the jump, and it was exhilarating.

This is a picture of faith: putting our whole weight on Jesus and his love for us. Looking back this is what I experienced in those years of illness. Up till that point I had known that God loved me, but there were lots of other things that I was relying on for my sense of worth, security and happiness. But when I got ill and these support structures were removed, I had to put my whole weight on Jesus Christ and his love for me. I had nothing else to lean on.

This is faith in Jesus Christ. You may have been going through life trusting in your own abilities and strengths, but there comes a point where you find that all you can do is put your whole weight on the only one who can secure you, hold you and love you perfectly.

FAITH AND REASON

We do not always understand why God asks us to do what he asks us to do, but faith is trusting in God's love and goodness. Abraham did not know where was going, but he trusted God. He did not know how he would be able to have a son in his old age, but he trusted God. He did not know why he should sacrifice his son, when his son was the fulfilment of a promise, but he trusted God.

This is not an irrational decision. It is really the most rational, sensible and reasonable thing you can ever do. For it means ceasing to rely on your strength and relying instead on the one who is Almighty God, no longer trusting in your understanding but trusting instead in the one who knows all things and understands all things, and putting yourself into the hands of one who loves you totally.

This is only possible because he loves you. His love makes it safe to put your faith in him. And then faith becomes the way in which you receive God's love. Love makes faith possible. Faith makes love real within us.

Here love and faith begin to work together in a virtuous circle, for God's love for us means that we can trust him, and as we trust him, we experience more of his love, which gives us greater confidence to trust him in all things. This is what we see in the life of Abraham, whose steps of faith grew every time. And this is what each of us can experience as we learn, step by step, to trust in the love of God.

As you receive this love, things begin to change in you. Which leads us to the impact of God's love for us.

PART THREE

The Impact of the Love of God

ROMANS 5–8

Chapter 6

CLOSER

*Therefore, since we have been justified through faith, we have
peace with God through our Lord Jesus Christ.*

ROMANS 5:1

'You were more intimately present to me than my innermost
being, and higher than the highest peak of my spirit.'*

ST AUGUSTINE

We were made for connection. There is something within us that
wants to know and be known, that craves intimacy and that needs
to be close to another person. It's the reason why loneliness is so
painful, why we fear being abandoned, and why social distancing
and lockdowns during 2020–2022 have been so damaging to our
souls.

And we desire *real* connection. Modern forms of communication, particularly social media, have enabled us to have some
connection in the form of the exchange of information. We can
send messages, watch videos, see photos, even do video calls, but it
is connection from a distance. And it always feels inadequate. Real
connection is loving people up close. This is what we long for.

We long for it, but we also fear it. For with closeness comes the
ability to be hurt or to hurt the other person. On one of our first
dates, I went to put my arm round Tara to draw her closer to me, but
in the act of trying to get my arm over her head I almost elbowed
her in the face. She had to duck out the way. I almost literally hurt

---

* St Augustine, *Confessions*, R.S. Pine-Coffin, Penguin Classics, 2003, 3.6.11.

her as I tried to be closer to her. Remarkably, we both still had a lovely evening.

We fear being abandoned or taken advantage of. And so, at the same time as we seek connection, we also avoid letting anyone get close to us. Some of us become clingy, afraid of being unloved or abandoned, worrying constantly about the state of our relationships. Others of us become avoidant, keeping everyone at a distance, avoiding vulnerability, resisting being close or depending on others.

In Romans 5, Paul claims that this desire for closeness, intimacy and connection is now fulfilled in our relationship with God, for 'since we have been justified through faith, we have *peace* with God through our Lord Jesus Christ' (5:1). The first consequence of God's love for us is that it establishes a relationship with himself. You are connected to the one source of perfect love in a relationship that is more significant than that of your parents or your children, your friends or a spouse. For it is the closest possible relationship you can ever be in.

PEACE WITH GOD

At the time Paul was writing his letter, the Church in Rome was living in the first century of the *Pax Romana* ('the peace of Rome'). The Emperor Augustus had managed to bring an end to years of civil war and establish peace across the empire, and he had achieved this through political power and military force. But Paul wanted to remind the Christians in Rome that they had a greater peace, one that had come through the work of Jesus Christ dying on a cross at the order of a Roman official in the corner of the empire. However, this peace is far more significant, powerful, and longer lasting.

By 'peace' Paul means a close, healthy, restored relationship. It does not refer to a peaceful feeling, but a relationship without barriers or distance. When you love someone, you want them to be close to you. God loves you and wants to be close to you. The result of being 'justified by faith' (put right in your relationship with God) is that all barriers in your relationship with God are removed. All the things that get in the way of any relationship with anyone, like anger, hostility, guilt, mistrust, deception, have been destroyed, and you can come close.

CLOSER

The story of the Bible is a story of a God who longs to be close to us. This is the reason for Creation: so that we might be with God. It is the tragedy of the Fall: the loss of intimacy with God. This is the whole narrative of the Bible: God trying to restore relationship with his people. This is the message of Christmas: the birth of one called Immanuel, God with Us. It is the characteristic of Jesus' ministry on earth: loving people close up, eating with them, touching the untouchable, sharing his life with those on the margins. It is the achievement of the cross: clearing every obstacle so that we could be close to God. It is the consequence of Pentecost: God's Spirit poured into our hearts. And it is our final destiny: the closest possible relationship with God forever.

The history of humanity's relationship with God has been our attempt to keep God at a distance, hiding, pretending, denying, and running. God has pursued peace with us; we have responded with hostility to him. It seems that we want independence more than connection, even though this ends up hurting us and ruining our lives. But the history of God's interaction with humanity has been his refusal to give up on us or let us go. God has been at work from the start to bring us close again. This has been the Father's desire: the longing for his children to come home. This has been the Son's achievement: dying on a cross in order to clear the way. This is what the Spirit has fulfilled: drawing us into the very life of God.

This kind of 'peace', connection with and closeness to God, is now available to each of us. But there are some obstacles. For a start you might feel like God cannot be trusted. Does he really love me? Is he good for me? But God's love has been 'demonstrated' through the cross. On the one hand this is clear evidence of the *reality* of God's love (he really does love us if he was willing to die for us in such a way), and on the other it is revelation of the *nature* of God's love as selfless, self-sacrificial, gracious. This is not a love to be afraid of.

The other objection is whether God will really love you, knowing as he does what you are really like. This is the fear at the heart of so many of our relationships (or lack of them): won't they just reject me when they discover what we are really like?

But God knows you and loves you. He sees you better than you see yourself. And he still loves you. Closeness with anyone comes when you allow them to see who you really are, and when you allow them to love you as you really are. This is the most frightening thing we can do, but it is also the most beautiful, healing, and transformative thing that we can do. It often feels impossible. It is far safer to love at a distance, to pretend we are better, stronger, or braver than we really are. But closeness with God, just as closeness with anyone else, comes from allowing God to see us as we are and for him to love us as we are.

This can be the most challenging and wonderful thing about marriage (or any close community). For in marriage there is no hiding. You allow someone to come into your life and see all your selfishness and weakness, and let them love you for who you are.

This is the beauty of confession, when we say to God, 'This is what I've done and this is who I really am, and I'm going to let you love me even so.' Confession is the process of allowing God to love the unlovable parts of us, allowing God to accept the very things that I reject in myself.

Paul says the same thing three times, in three different ways: 'When we were still powerless, Christ died for the ungodly' (5:6), 'While we were still sinners Christ died for us' (5:8), and 'While we God's were enemies, we were reconciled to him through the death of his Son' (5:10). When we were at our worst, God loved us most.

When we were weakest, God's love was strongest. When we were most hostile to God, God's love was most gracious to us. When we were furthest away, God's love brought us closer than ever.

You might think that the worst parts of you keep God away, when they are the very things that can draw him close.

Once we had a knock on the door from a neighbour to tell us that sewage was flowing out of our drains on to the road towards his house. This was the first time we had met him, and I immediately became apologetic, imagining that he would be angry. But he was very friendly, for he explained that he was a plumber, and he was offering to come and fix the problem. So, we invited him in and he fixed our drains for us.

Something I assumed would push a neighbour away (our sewage moving towards his house), was something that brought him closer, because he was uniquely qualified to deal with the problem we were facing. God is uniquely qualified to deal with the mess and chaos of our lives. He is the one who forgives sins, heals hurts, restores brokenness, comforts our pain, guides us in our lostness and turns our darkness into light.

When we read the Gospels, it is not the good and the clean whom Jesus draws close to. It is the dirty, the sick, the outcasts, the ones who are aware of the mess in their lives. Jesus connects with them through these things, forgiving sins, cleansing sickness, raising the dead.

The Apostle James writes, 'Come near to God and he will come near to you'*. You can have peace with God. You can be connected to the one for whom you were made. For God loves you and longs to be close to you, if only you will let him.

---

* James 4:8.

Chapter 7

HOPE

… we know that suffering produces perseverance; perseverance, character; and character, hope. And hope does not put us to shame, because God's love has been poured out into our hearts through the Holy Spirit, who has been given to us.

ROMANS 5:3–5

'Few will have the greatness to bend history itself, but each of us can work to change a small portion of events. It is from numberless acts of courage and belief that human history is shaped. Each time a man stands up for an ideal, or acts to improve the lot of others, or strikes out against injustice, he sends forth a tiny ripple of hope, and crossing each other from a million different centres of energy and daring those ripples build a current which can sweep down the mightiest walls of oppression and resistance.'*

ROBERT F. KENNEDY

We face health issues, work issues or relationship issues where it seems like there is no solution. We have dreams and ambitions which feel impossible. We may have friends, family members, colleagues who are facing situations that seem so desperate that we don't know what to say to them. And then there are global situations – conflict, poverty, inequality, injustice, climate change, pandemics – and it looks like nothing could ever change or will ever change.

* Robert F. Kennedy, quoted in *The Assassination of Robert F. Kennedy*, Jacqueline Ching, Rosen Publishing Group, 2001, p30.

In the face of these things, we can either fall into despair (which is where we lose all hope) or denial (where we try to pretend that things aren't as bad as they seem). If we despair, we give up on anything ever changing for us or for others. We become cynical and demotivated. If we fall into denial, we fail to address the problems within us or around us, becoming superficial and detached from reality.

But hope is where we acknowledge the difficulties of our situation, but believe that something can change. Hope means facing the harsh reality of our lives, but also believing that there is a greater reality. Hope is knowing the complexities of the story we are in, but having confidence that it is not the end of the story. Hope is neither optimism nor pessimism. It is not thinking things are better than they are, or worse than they are. It connects us to the pain in the world, but also promises something beyond the pain.

And it is God's love for us that makes hope possible. The basis of hope for your life is not your circumstances, or your own ability to change things, but the love of God. Hope is personal. In the Bible the people of God often cry out to him, saying, 'Our hope is in you.'* Hope is based on knowing that you are loved by a God who can turn around any situation.

AS GOOD AS DEAD

At the end of Romans 4, Paul reminds the Church in Rome about Abraham's apparently hopeless situation. He faced the bitter disappointment of not having any children, and Paul says that he 'faced the fact that his body was as good as dead' (4:19). You might feel, similarly, that a relationship is as good as dead, or your job prospects are as good as dead, or your social life is as good as dead, or the dreams you once had for your life are as good as dead.

This is a vital first step towards having hope. For real hope requires us to face the facts of our situation. Hope is not self-

* See Jeremiah 14:22.

delusion. Abraham faced the facts of his inability to have children. He was not ignorant of the basic laws of nature. He knew that it was impossible for him and his wife to have children at their age. He saw the reality of his situation, but he also saw a different reality: the reality of the love of God. This is hope, where we see both the facts of our situation but also the truth of a God who loves us and can transform any situation.

This hope builds our character. Paul writes that 'we also rejoice in our sufferings, because we know that suffering produces perseverance; perseverance, character; and character, hope' (5:3–4). So, Paul seems to be saying that hope comes as the final stage in the process of suffering leading to perseverance, which leads to growth in character, which leads to growing in hope. However, Paul has already mentioned hope in verse 2, so I wonder if Paul is describing something that is circular, not linear. It is a virtuous circle created by hope.

> We rejoice in the hope of the glory of God. Not only so but we also rejoice in our sufferings, because we know that suffering produces perseverance; perseverance, character; and character, hope.

ROMANS 5:2–4

When difficulty comes into your life, hope enables you to keep going, which grows your character, which creates more hope. Hope is the key element that transforms our experience of suffering, producing perseverance, and character, and more hope.

This hope gives us perseverance. Hope keeps us loving and keeps us believing. This hope gives us courage. Asking someone out on a date, being the first to say I love you, proposing, applying to university or for a job, trying to set up your own company or your own charity, standing for elected office, are all acts of hope. It's easy to be cynical or negative, but hope is courageous. This hope changes the world.

And hope grows within us as we grow in our knowledge of God's love for us.

THE PROMISES OF THE FATHER

Our hope grows from the loving promises of God the Father. Abraham had hope because of what God had said to him.

> *When everything was hopeless, Abraham believed anyway, deciding to live not on the basis of what he saw he* couldn't *do, but on what God said he* would *do.*

ROMANS 4:18, MSG

There are the general promises of God which we find in the Bible. These are given to all of us: that he will never leave or forsake us, that he will forgive all our sins, always love us.* But there are also specific promises which you may feel God has given to you, which gives you hope for specific situations. This was the case with Abraham who had a specific promise from God that he would have a son.

Tara and I initially struggled to have children. We had a couple of disappointments, and things just didn't seem to be happening for us. But on 17th October 2010, Tara read the story of Elisha and the Shunnanite woman** and when she read the verses where Elisha said to the woman, 'About this time next year … you will hold a son', it jumped out at her, and it felt like God was saying the same thing to her. She held on to it as a promise from God for us too. This verse gave us hope over the coming months and on 18th October 2011, exactly a year and a day after she had read that story and held on to that promise, she held in her arms a son, our first child, Albie.

God's promises give us hope. There may be delays, but we know he loves us and he is faithful in his promises.

---

* Deuteronomy 31:6, Psalm 103:3, Jeremiah 31:3.
** 2 Kings 4:16.

My mother has been an amazing mother in almost every way, and far be from me to criticize anything she did as we grew up. However, she was quite often late collecting us from school. We would normally be the last children in the playground at the end of the school day. But we never doubted she would come to get us, because she'd said she'd be there, and she loved us. Whether I'd had a good day or a bad day at school, I knew she had promised to be there and I knew that she would come.

It is the same with God. You will have good days and bad days. There may be times where it feels like God is delaying, but he will always come for you because that's what he's promised to do, because he loves you.

THE ACTION OF THE SON

In addition to the loving words of the Father we also have the loving actions of the Son, which give us hope. Our hope is based on the death and resurrection of Jesus.

I have often wondered why the English are so hopeful every four years when we approach another football World Cup. It rarely matches either the current reality or past experience, and yet we seem to have this irrational hope that we just might win this time. I think our irrational hope stems from the fact that in 1966 England won the World Cup, and that event affected the collective psyche of a whole nation. I'm sure we wouldn't feel as hopeful if we'd never won, but ever since 1966, whenever we approach a tournament, no matter how bad things appear, we know that it has happened before and so it can happen again.

In the New Testament, before Jesus' death and resurrection, there is very little mention of hope in the New Testament. We don't even find hope mentioned by name in the Gospels. However, after the resurrection everything changes. The writings of the first

Christians become characterized by hope because something has happened that has changed their entire worldview.

The death and resurrection of Jesus Christ is a source of hope because, the cross shows us that there is nothing that God would not do for us, and the resurrection shows us there's nothing that God cannot do for us. Our hope is based on the fact that God loves us, and God can act to help us. The cross is the eternal demonstration of God's love for us. The resurrection is the eternal proof of God's power to change things. These events give us hope, because they show that God has both the motivation and the ability to act for us. They reassure us that sin and death do not have the last word, that God can turn the worst things in history into the best things, that God can do anything, that there are no limits to the extent of his love and the power of his love.

Bishop Lesslie Newbigin was once asked whether he was an optimist or a pessimist. He replied, 'I am neither an optimist nor a pessimist. I believe that Jesus Christ is risen from the dead.' This is the guarantee that you can have hope.

THE PRESENCE OF THE HOLY SPIRIT

Finally, this love which is communicated through the loving words of the Father, and the loving actions of the Son, is also experienced through the loving presence of the Holy Spirit. Paul writes, 'And hope does not put us to shame, because God's love has been poured into our hearts through the Holy Spirit, who has been given to us' (5:5). Our hope grows not only from an objective, historical event, but also from a subjective, personal experience of God's love in our hearts. Hope*less*ness comes from feeling alone; hope*ful*ness comes from experiencing God's presence.

There is a kind of hope that comes just by someone being with us. The circumstances might not change, but we have someone with us, so we are not alone. But the Holy Spirit is more than a reassuring presence. He is God himself, the one who raised Jesus from the dead, through whom Jesus healed the sick and drove out demons. He is the presence of one who can turn the impossible into the possible.

These are all signs of God's love for you. The Father makes promises to you because he loves you. Jesus died for you because he loves you and there is nothing he would not do for you. The Spirit has come to live within you because he loves you. And so, as one deeply loved, you can have hope.

PERMANENT, PERVASIVE AND PERSONAL

In the 1970s, psychologists were developing theories about what caused people to feel helpless and give up hope. They discovered that if the problems that people experienced felt *permanent* ('this thing isn't going to go away'), *pervasive* ('it's going to ruin everything') and *personal* ('this kind of stuff always happens to me'), then they would become helpless. They believed that if you could only get people to see their difficulties as less permanent ('this isn't going to last forever'), less pervasive ('this isn't going to affect every aspect of my life') and less personal ('this happens to lots of people, not just me'), they would become less helpless.

There may well be a lot of truth in this approach. However, God restores our hope by offering us something which is *more permanent, more pervasive* and *more personal* than anything else we might experience. God's love is permanent, because God promises always to love you. Nothing is as permanent as the love of God. It is eternal, unfailing, steadfast, unchanging. It is pervasive, because it affects every part of your life – your heart and mind, your body and soul, your private life and your public life, your relationships and your work, your past and present and future. Nothing is as pervasive as the love of God. And it is personal, because God loves not just humanity in general, but you in particular. For Jesus is the

Good Shepherd who leaves the ninety-nine to go after the one who is lost, who spots the individual from the crowd, and would have died for you if you were the only person in the universe. God's love is not an impersonal force, or a universal principle, but a personal connection to you, whom he knows and loves.

This is the hope that comes from being loved by God.

Chapter 8

JOY

We rejoice in the hope of the glory of God ... We also rejoice in our sufferings ... We also rejoice in God through our Lord Jesus Christ, through whom we have now received reconciliation.

ROMANS 5:11, ESV

'You do not look so happy as I mean you to be.'*

ASLAN

God loves you and he wants you to be happy.

When you love someone, it is natural that you want that person to be happy. As a husband who loves his wife, I want my wife to be happy. As a father who loves his children, I want my children to be happy. As a friend who loves my friends, I want my friends to be happy. Love always desires the happiness of the beloved, and God, who loves us most, most desires our happiness.

Not only this, but God also has the capacity to make you happy. There is no one who wants your happiness more, and there is no one who has greater ability to make you happy than the God who loves you.

CIRCUMSTANCES, EXPERIENCES, RELATIONSHIPS, SELVES

We tend to look for happiness in four main places. Firstly, we seek happiness from the circumstances of our lives: where we live, the

---

* C. S. Lewis, *The Last Battle*, HarperCollins, 2014, p221.

work we do, the environment around us. Secondly, we look for happiness through what we experience: what we eat, what we watch, the things we do. Thirdly, we look for happiness through people and relationships; from romance, friendship, family, or meeting someone interesting on a bus. Finally, we can try to become the source of our own happiness, either through a process of self-improvement (like trying to lose weight) or through self-acceptance (like trying to be happy with our present weight).

Now many of these things are good and can be genuine sources of happiness. It really does make me happy when I'm in the middle of a good book, or when my children tell me that they love me, and I was extremely happy when England beat Australia in the Rugby World Cup final in 2003.

However, none of these things are capable of being the source of our ultimate happiness. They are imperfect, temporary and do not have the capacity to touch the deepest parts of our beings that long for true, lasting happiness. The book finishes, there is an argument at home, and the English rugby team went through a prolonged slump after their World Cup success.

Things start going wrong when we look to these things as the ultimate basis of our happiness. We become restless and frustrated with the circumstances of our lives, thinking that if we could only get the right job, the right house, in the right location, once we've done the extension, and got the right government, then we will be happy. Or we begin to chase more and more positive experiences, avoiding or suppressing pain and difficulty. We move from taking pleasure in good things, to seeking increasingly strong experiences that are never quite enough.

And we can start expecting too much from other people. We hope that a partner, or a child, or a particular group of friends will secure our happiness, thinking that maybe their affection, their affirmation, their need for us and love for us will make us completely happy. But one of the most important lessons to learn in any relationship is that you cannot be the source of another's happiness. And to place that expectation on another is to place them under unbearable pressure. Some of us want others to be happy, and to be the source of that happiness. Others of us want to be happy ourselves, but need others to be the source of our happiness. Both attempts are equally futile and dangerous. Looking for happiness in our relationships can cause us to flit from person to person, hoping that this next group, or next partner, might be the one finally to make us happy. The promise of 'happily ever after' can never be found in another person.

Nor can we become the ultimate source of happiness for ourselves. We become caught in the tension between self-improvement and self-acceptance, recognizing that it is very difficult to have both simultaneously. Our attempts at self-improvement either fail, or don't give us what we were looking for. And our efforts at self-acceptance struggle to eliminate words of doubt or criticism. But most of all, just as hoping another person might make us happy will end up with disappointment, so too will trying to be the source of our own happiness. For the very things that prevent us from being the source of happiness for another person (our imperfections), prevents us from being the source of our own happiness.

There is only one who is able to make you truly happy, and he is able to give you something deeper and greater than happiness: joy.

LOVE AND JOY

Three times in Romans 5:1–11, as Paul describes the consequences of God's love for us, he says 'we rejoice'. First, 'we rejoice in the hope of the glory of God' (5:2); then 'we rejoice in our sufferings' (5:3), and finally, 'we rejoice in God through our Lord Jesus Christ through whom we have received reconciliation' (5:11). John Stott, commenting on this section of Romans, wrote, 'It seems clear from this paragraph, then, that the major mark of justified believers is joy, especially joy in God himself.'*

* John Stott, *The Message of Romans*, IVP, 1994, p148.

Joy is something more than happiness. The times in my life when I think I have felt this joy most fully have been the times when it has broken through the unhappiness, when I've been homesick, heartbroken, lonely, or depressed, and yet it feels like there is something solid 'beneath' all the other real feelings, which is joy. It is deeper than our circumstances, or our successes, or our failures. It is based on a new situation that has been created: reconciliation, justification, peace with God.

It is stronger than happiness. This joy is not fragile or transient. In the Old Testament Nehemiah tells the people of God, that 'the joy of the LORD is your strength.' At that time the Israelites were weak. Their walls were destroyed, they were surrounded by enemies, and facing huge issues of poverty and instability, but the joy of the Lord gave them a strength to overcome the challenges they were facing.

The message of Christianity is a message of joy. At the first Christmas Mary declared, 'my spirit *rejoices* in God my Saviour' when she was told she would bear the Messiah, and the shepherds were told of 'good news that will cause great *joy*' that Jesus had been born. At the first Easter Jesus rose from the dead, conquering sin, death and suffering, and the disciples were '*overjoyed* when they saw the Lord'. At the first Pentecost, God poured out his Spirit on the first Christians and they were filled with joy. The fruit of the Spirit being in our lives is first love, and second joy. And at the end of all things Jesus will return, completing the work he has started, and Revelation promises, '"He will wipe every tear from their eyes. There will be no more death" or mourning or crying or pain, for the old order of things has passed away."* It will be joy forever.

This is the character of the Christian faith. If Christians or the Church have ever been associated with gloom or joylessness, it has only been due to a failure of the Church to grasp the reality of the love of God. Christianity is a religion of joy because it is a religion

---

* Nehemiah 8:10, Luke 1:47 [emphasis added], Luke 2:10, John 20:20 [emphasis added], Galatians 5:22, Revelation 21:4.

of love. There is no greater joy than knowing that you are truly and deeply loved. In fact, it is the only source of true joy. And it is a joy that is deeper, stronger, longer lasting and more abundant than anything this world can offer.

And we find this joy in three ways.

In Hope

First, 'we rejoice in hope' (5:2). This joy is based on what *has happened* (the cross and resurrection) but also on what *will happen* (future salvation). Our joy is like that of an engagement. When a couple gets engaged there is joy, partly in recognition of the couple's love for each other (hopefully) in the present, but more in anticipation of what is to come in the future. In the same way, our joy is based partly on what we already experience in our relationship with God, but also because of what is to come, the perfection of our relationship with God forever.

In the meantime there will always be sadness and anxiety, tragedies and disappointment, heartbreak and despair. But there is a joy that comes from the hope that this is not the end, and there is a 'happily ever after' for everyone who believes.

In Sufferings

We also 'rejoice in our sufferings' (5:3). This joy is not found by avoiding pain or difficulty. Living in the love of God makes us both happier and sadder. We are happier because we know that we are loved unconditionally and abundantly. We are sadder because we are also connected to the pain of the world more deeply. God's love within us should mean that we feel greater compassion for those who are hurting, more anger at injustice, more sadness that the world is not as it should be.

As a father I desperately want my children to be happy, but I know that I must not therefore try to protect them from experiencing anything sad or painful. Instead, I want to give them a deep sense of joy rooted in the knowledge that they are unconditionally loved.

The Psalms, which command us more than anywhere else in the Bible to rejoice, also contain more than anywhere the emotions of despair, sadness, grief and anger. For the love of God draws us into a life of both the heights and the depths.

In his book, *A Severe Mercy*, Sheldon Vanauken describes how, aged fifteen, he came to realize the source of true joy and that it came with a decision he had to make.

> How did one find joy? In the books it seemed to be found in love – a great love … So, if he wanted the heights of joy, he must have, if he could find it, a great love. But in the books again, great joy through love seemed always to go hand in hand with frightful pain. Still, he thought, looking out across the meadow, still, the joy would be worth the pain – if, indeed, they went together. If there were a choice – and he suspected there was – a choice between, on the one hand, the heights and the depths and, on the other hand, some sort of safe, cautious middle way, he for one, here and now chose the heights and the depths.*

And Sheldon Vanauken certainly experienced both the heights and the depths in his life, and later in life affirmed that 'the joy *was* worth the pain'. What he did not know then, but later discovered through his friendship with C.S. Lewis, was the origin of the greatest love, and that the joy could be eternal.

In the Love of God

Finally, 'we rejoice in God' (5:11). Our joy is found in a relationship, the one relationship that can make us truly happy. This is the reason God commands us to rejoice so many times in the Bible, for he is commanding us to find our happiness in the only one who truly satisfies our desire for joy. We find our joy in the God who loves us.

This joy comes from the *depth* of God's love. Paul writes that 'love of God has been poured into our *hearts* through the Holy Spirit' (5:5). The 'heart' refers to the centre of who we are. There are

---

* Sheldon Vanauken, *A Severe Mercy*, Hodder and Stoughton, 1979, p18.

all kinds of things that hurt and discourage us, and some things can go in deep, creating a deep pain. But the love of God goes deeper than anything else, and can give us a deep joy, even in our pain.

This joy comes from the *abundance* of God's love. For this love is '*poured* into our hearts' (5:5). Eugene Peterson translates it as 'we can't round up enough containers to hold everything God generously pours into our lives through the Holy Spirit!'* Twice in these verses Paul uses the phrase 'how much more', for however much we've done wrong or been wronged, the love of God is more. Sometimes we lose our joy when we feel overwhelmed by all the problems in our lives, by the sheer volume of what we are facing. But the love of God is more abundant than all the things that can rob us of our joy.

This joy comes from the *certainty* of God's love. The word 'rejoice' might better be translated 'have joyful confidence'. And we can be sure that we are loved, because God has *demonstrated* his love for us on the cross (5:8). The cross is the sign of God's love. So many things in our lives are uncertain, and these uncertainties can cause fear and anxiety, but there is one thing that is absolutely certain: God's love for us.

And this joy comes from the *permanence* of God's love. The pleasures of this world are temporary, but the joy on offer to us is based on something permanent, and unconditional. For this is a love that embraces us at our worst, for, 'while we were still sinners, Christ died for us' (5:8). This is where the deepest joy comes from.

A friend of mine told me about an occasion where his three-year-old son was really unhappy about everything, and started behaving incredibly badly. He was hitting and shouting and screaming and throwing things. He was throwing toys, throwing books, throwing clothes. He said he'd never seen this child so angry or behave so badly. In the middle of this rage, my friend picked the child up and

---

* Romans 5:5, MSG.

carried him to his room to try to contain him there, but the boy started trying to wreck the room. Meanwhile, my friend sat calmly on the child's bed and waited until the child collapsed in a heap from exhaustion. He then picked him up and put him in his lap and said to him, 'I love you.' And the child replied, 'Well, I don't love you.' Then my friend said to him, 'You may not love me, but I still love you and I will always love you. You've done some bad things this evening, but that doesn't stop me loving you, and no matter what you do throughout the rest of your life nothing can ever stop me loving you.' After that the boy paused, then looked up at his father and said, 'I love you a little bit' and the father said that he saw a spark of the beginnings of joy returning to his boy.

At the very end of C.S. Lewis' *The Last Battle*, Aslan looks at the children and says, 'You do not yet look so happy as I mean you to be.'* This is how God looks at you and me. You are not as happy as he means you to be. Maybe it's because you have been looking to other things to give you a happiness that only he can give. Maybe it's because you don't trust that he really wants you to be happy. But I am convinced that the answer is found in the love of God. For the most joyful people are those who know that they are most loved. And the most joyful life is one in which we live in the knowledge of the greatest love there is.

* Lewis, *The Last Battle*, p221.

Chapter 9

LIFE

Consequently, just as one trespass resulted in condemnation for all people, so also one righteous act resulted in justification and life for all people.

ROMANS 5:18

'She sang of the Love that is perfected by death, of the Love that dies not in the tomb.'*

OSCAR WILDE

God's love for you is permanent. He will never give up loving you. He will love you forever. And therefore, God's love is stronger than death.

Death is life's great certainty. It is unavoidable and hangs over our lives. We will all die and all those we love will die. This is the problem of physical death. But there is also spiritual death, which might be less apparent but is just as real. For there are things that can happen to us – disappointments, rejections, tragedies – which seem to drain the life out of us. There also are things that we do – selfishness, pride, bitterness – which can make us feel less alive. We can be physically alive, but feel like something has died within us spiritually.

But the love of God brings us back to life. It has the power to overcome both physical death and spiritual death. This is a love that makes us more alive in the present and promises eternal life

* Oscar Wilde, 'The Nightingale and the Rose', *Collins Complete Works of Oscar Wilde*, HarperCollins, 1999, p281.

in the future.

In Romans 5, Paul contrasts sin, condemnation and death on the one hand with grace ('the gift'), justification and life on the other:

> *But the gift is not like the trespass. For if the many died by the trespass of the one man, how much more did God's grace and the gift that came by the grace of the one man, Jesus Christ, overflow to the many! Nor can the gift of God be compared with the result of one man's sin: The judgment followed one sin and brought condemnation, but the gift followed many trespasses and brought justification. For if, by the trespass of the one man, death reigned through that one man, how much more will those who receive God's abundant provision of grace and of the gift of righteousness reign in life through the one man, Jesus Christ!*
>
> *Consequently, just as one trespass resulted in condemnation for all people, so also one righteous act resulted in justification and life for all people. For just as through the disobedience of the one man the many were made sinners, so also through the obedience of the one man the many will be made righteous.*

ROMANS 5:15-19

Paul is saying that in Jesus Christ, grace is stronger than sin, justification is stronger than condemnation, and life is stronger than death. Jesus has turned sin to grace, condemnation to justification, and death to life. And this 'life' is both spiritual life and eternal life.

SPIRITUAL LIFE

You are not yet as alive as God intends you to be. St Irenaeus said, 'The glory of God is a human being fully alive.' The problem is that we are not yet 'fully alive'.

In this part of Romans, Paul refers to the story of Adam and Eve in the Garden of Eden, where death enters the world as a result of human sin. This is not only the origin of physical death, but also spiritual death. For sin separates us from the God who is the source of all life, so every time we sin something dies within us. We might remain physically alive, but spiritually we are dying.

But the love of God brings us back to life. Paul writes that the result of one act of righteousness was justification that *brings life* for all people (5:18). Justification refers to our restored status before God, the putting right of our relationship with him. And this is a relationship that gives us life. It makes us more fully alive.

Some relationships cause us to lose confidence, making us feel less ourselves; other relationships build us up, and make us more confident, enabling us to feel more alive. And our relationship with God is one that makes us more, not less. God's love restores us, replenishes us, refreshes us, and revitalizes us. He is the living God and when we are connected to the living God, his life flows into our lives.

Love creates life. This happens on a biological level, where new human beings are (ideally) created in the context of love. And this happens on a spiritual level when we are loved by God.

We see this in each person of the Trinity. The Father's love brings us life. In the story of the Prodigal Son, when the son returns home to his father, his father runs to him and embraces him, kisses him, and gives him a ring, and sandals and a robe. Then the father says, 'For this son of mine was dead and is *alive* again; he was lost and is found.'*

We see this in God the Son, Jesus Christ. Jesus came to bring us back to life. John's Gospel proclaims, 'in him was *life*, and that life was the light of all mankind.'** It doesn't mean that Jesus was simply physically alive, but that there was an abundance of life within him. Jesus was and is the most fully alive human being who has ever lived, flowing out of his perfect relationship with God the Father, who is the source of all life. And now Jesus has come to give us that

* Luke 15:24 [emphasis added].
** John 1:4 [emphasis added].

same life. He said, 'I have come that you might have life and life in all its fullness." Jesus makes us more alive. He came into the world not just to make bad people good; he came to make dead people alive. He is the Resurrection and the Life."

And we see this in God the Holy Spirit, for 'the Spirit gives life."" The Spirit of God is the one who is with us in the darkest times, even when we are surrounded by death. In the Psalms David holds on to this, 'Even though I walk through the valley of the shadow of death, I will fear no evil for you are with me.""

ETERNAL LIFE

God's love makes us more alive *spiritually*, but it also guarantees us life *eternally*.

The hope of life after death in the New Testament is not based on a belief in the immortality of the soul (that some part of us cannot die and so must live on); it is based on a confidence in God's love for us being more powerful even than death. Just as, though Jesus died on a cross, God's love for him caused him to raise him to new life, so when we die God's love for us will cause him to raise us to new life.

God's love for Jesus didn't make him immune to suffering, disappointment, rejection or even death. But it meant that God held him through these things and brought him out to life the other side. It's the same for us. The love of God holds us in the troubles and tragedies of this life and carries us into new life beyond the grave.

This love reassures us that life is stronger than death. Dead relationships can be brought back to life, dead dreams can be brought back to life, dead churches can be brought back to life, and dead bodies can be brought back to life.

* John 10:10.
** John 11:25.
*** 2 Corinthians 3:6.
**** Psalm 23:4.

In April 2015 Tara and I went to Jerusalem, and visited Yad Vashem, the Holocaust Memorial Museum. The museum walks through the whole history of the Holocaust, and we felt overwhelmed when confronted by the horrific extent of so many deaths and by the evil ideology of Nazi Germany which at one time was so powerful. Right at the end of the tour we came to the Hall of Remembrance, where the museum has tried to collect as much information as possible about every person who died in the Holocaust. Next to the Hall is a little side room, where you can sit down at a computer and look up anyone who may have died during the Holocaust. So, Tara and I went into this little room, and typed in 'Gumbel' to see what would come up. Our eyes filled with tears as we read the names of Anna Gumbel who died in Riga in 1941, Emma Gumbel who died in Theresienstadt in Czechoslovakia in 1942, Gottfreid Gumbel who died in the same concentration camp in 1943 and Siegfried Gumbel who died in Dachau in 1942.

We were being confronted by the death of my relatives by an evil regime, and yet as we sat there we knew that Tara was pregnant with our third child. Had that regime been successful in its aims there would now be no Gumbels in the world at all. But there in Jerusalem, Tara was sitting next to me about to produce yet another Gumbel child. Despite the overwhelming and incomprehensible evil of the Holocaust, death had not been allowed to have the last word. More and more Gumbels are being born, and life continues.

The more you love someone the more time you want to have with them. And God's love for us is infinite, and so for him our lifetime is not enough time with us. His eternal love for us desires eternity with us. 'God so loved the world that he gave his only Son, that whoever believes in him shall not perish but have eternal life.'* The reason God created eternal life is so that he might be able to love us forever.

* John 3:16.

LIVING IN LOVE

God's love means that life is stronger than death. But here we discover a paradox. For we receive this life by dying. Jesus died in order that we might have life, and then this becomes the model for our lives. We die with Christ and are raised to new life. To become a Christian is not an attempt to add 10% to your existing life. It means dying to your old life and being raised to new life. Jesus said, 'whoever wants to save their life will lose it, but whoever loses their life for me and for the gospel will find it.'*

This may sound extreme but embracing anything new or different always involves dying to something. A healthy relationship means dying to selfishness, community means dying to independence, fitness means dying to inactivity, health means dying to donuts, honesty means dying to pride. And becoming a Christian requires us to die to ourselves in order that we might receive eternal life.

A friend of mine went out to work with St Stephen's Society in Hong Kong, giving up her life and friends in the UK, to share the good news of the love of God with those she lived with there. She had no income, very little time to herself, working in a context where she didn't know the language, and had almost no control over her life. She said of that time, 'It's the hardest thing I've ever done. But I've never felt more fully alive.'

And God's eternal, undying love makes it all worth it. There may be all kinds of things you have to give up in this life, even things that feel precious and essential. But it is possible because you have a love which will never end.

In Romans 5:17 Paul again uses the phrase 'how much more' to describe the extent of God's grace and life for us. There is a Greek word which Paul could have used which means 'abound, surpass, overflow'. But this word is apparently insufficient for what he wants to articulate. Instead, he uses a word which means 'to exist in even

* Mark 8:35.

greater abundance'. Though sin and death came through Adam, the restored relationship and life that comes through Jesus Christ exists in even greater abundance. Grace is so much stronger than sin. Justification is so much stronger than condemnation. Your future is so much more promising than your past. And God's love is so much stronger than death.

And this turnaround comes through 'one man', Jesus Christ. In the world of romance people sometimes talk about looking for, or finding, 'the one'. What they seem to mean is that there is one person out there whom we are meant for, who will love us as we've always longed to be loved, and we will love them in return with the love we've always longed to give. They may not be perfect, but they will be perfect for us. The Bible is clear that there is 'the one' out there for you – whose love you have been searching for all your life. His name is Jesus Christ, who is perfect, who loves you perfectly, and whose love for you is the hope for eternal life.

Chapter 10

FREEDOM

Therefore, there is now no condemnation for those who are in Christ Jesus, because through Christ Jesus the law of the Spirit who gives life has set you free from the law of sin and death.

ROMANS 8:1–2

'The fruit of too much liberty is slavery.'*

CICERO

If there are things in your life which control you, you are not free. If I can't walk past a chocolate brownie without eating it, then that chocolate brownie controls me, and I am not truly free. If I cannot restrain myself from checking my phone to follow a sporting event when I am supposed to be listening to someone, then I am not truly free. If I am unable to say what I really think, or do what I really want to do, because I'm afraid of what people will think, then I am controlled by my fear and I'm not truly free. If I find myself always needing to conform to be like the people around me, then I am not truly free. And if I find myself always needing to be different to and disagree with other people even when they're right, then I'm not truly free.

Whenever habits, substances, people, fears or expectations control our lives it shows us that we are not free. You may live in a 'free country' where there is freedom of speech, freedom of expression, freedom of movement, and yet if these things control you, you are not truly free.

* Cicero, *The Republic*, 1.68.

The message of Christianity is one of total freedom: freedom from sin, freedom from guilt, freedom from shame, freedom from death, freedom from fear and freedom to be the people that deep down we long to be and were made to be.

The book of Exodus in the Old Testament tells the story of God liberating his people from slavery in Egypt. As Moses attempts to negotiate the freedom of his people, there are moments when Pharaoh offers him partial, or temporary, freedom. But Moses demands full and permanent freedom for the Israelites, refusing to give up until he achieves total freedom from slavery for his people.* In the same way, Jesus has come to set you free and will not give up until he has achieved your total liberation. This is freedom not just in one area of your life, or for one period of your life. It is total and eternal freedom. Jesus came to preach good news to the poor and to proclaim *freedom* for the captives, and declared, 'if the Son sets you free, you will be free indeed'.**

God's love not only sets us free, but it also enables us to be people who set others free. The same Spirit who anointed Jesus to proclaim freedom for the captives, anoints us to do the same. We are set free in order to bring freedom to others.

TWO KINDS OF SLAVERY

In Romans 6 and 7 Paul describes two obstacles to freedom: 'the Law' (which was the body of external requirements of how to live) and what he calls 'the sinful nature' (our internal struggles with things like selfishness, pride, bitterness and anger). Both the Law and the sinful nature stop us being free, and Jesus has the power to bring us freedom from each of them.

First there is the slavery that comes from 'the Law'. For Paul, 'the Law' was the written code of how to live recorded in the Old

* Exodus 5–11.
** Luke 4, John 8:36.

Testament. It was made up of 365 prohibitions (things we're not supposed to do) and 248 commandments (things we are supposed to do). The Law itself was given by God and is good. The Psalms talk of 'delighting' in the law of the Lord.* They are good laws, banning violence and exploitation, and requiring the care of the poor, and justice for everyone regardless of their sex or race or social position.

However, Paul explains that though the Law can define what sin is, and reveal the sin within us, it is limited, because it can neither rescue us from sin, nor remove it from us. And as we are never quite able to live up to the standard of the Law, always falling short, the Law becomes a burden for us. So, we find ourselves either pretending that we're doing better than we are, or we are filled with guilt and shame that we keep messing up. Whether it causes us to hide our struggles, or to be filled with shame, we are not truly free.

Then there is slavery to 'the sinful nature'. Within all of us are desires, impulses, and emotions which, though created good by God, are also fallen and corrupted. They can become selfish and self-destructive. We can find ourselves unable to resist the powerful internal desires within us even when we know that they are wrong, and so we are not free.

The theological term for being ruled by the Law is 'legalism'; being ruled by our sinful nature is called 'antinomianism'. Both are forms of slavery.

These two kinds of restrictions to our freedom are beautifully illustrated in Disney's *Frozen*.** The film has two central characters, Elsa and Anna, who are sisters and princesses. Elsa has some magical powers, which means that she can make snow and ice. This power can bring joy and delight, but it can also bring harm, and at a young age she nearly kills her sister. As a result of this she is told to repress this power and try to hold it in. She talks (and sometimes sings) to

* See Psalm 1:2.
** *Frozen*, directed by Chris Buck and Jennifer Lee, Walt Disney Pictures, 2013.

herself about trying not feel what she's feeling, and hiding instead. They lock the palace gates and she keeps everyone at a distance, including her sister Anna who loves her and doesn't understand why her sister keeps pushing her away. She is repressing her internal desires, trying to live up to external expectations, isolating herself from everyone. She is hurting her sister. She is alone. And she is not free.

However, after a few things go wrong she discovers that she cannot live this way, and decides to stop repressing these internal desires, marching off to the mountains and singing her famous song, *Let it go*,* in which she sings about the end of hiding and restraints. She abandons all restrictions and constraints, even those from morality ('no right, no wrong, no rules for me'), declaring that she is free. Instead of living according to external expectations, she is now living according to her desires.

She is claiming that she is now truly free, however the reality is different. Her decision to live according to her internal desires releases creativity and power, but causes destruction and pain for everyone around her, and the song ends with her slamming the door of her ice castle shut. She has swapped the closed gates of one castle for another, becoming even more removed from other people, and she's alone again.

Previously she kept people at a distance because of her repressed desires, but now she is isolated due to her decision to indulge her desires. Because if you want to do whatever you want, you have to be alone. Other people with their needs and desires act as a limit to what we can do, and relationships always require self-restraint on our part. So, when Anna comes to find Elsa, Elsa again pushes her sister away and does even more damage the second time. Theologically, she has moved from legalism to antinomianism, and she's still not free. She's still hurting the people around her.

* 'Let it go', written by Kristen Anderson-Lopez and Robert Lopez, performed by Idina Menzel in *Frozen*, Wonderland Music Company, 2013.

This has been the general movement of Western society in the last hundred years or so. At the beginning of the twentieth century, we lived in a society where there were many rules, expectations, and duties. It may have been restrictive, legalistic, and repressive, but arguably there was also a greater sense of responsibility, social cohesion, and community. Then after the Second World War there was a greater desire for freedom, being able to follow one's own desires and control one's own destiny. This has created many very good things, but with it has come individualism, the breakdown of community, and the rise of various kinds of addictions and compulsive behaviours. We are still looking for freedom.

LOVE AND FREEDOM

Freedom is not found in repressing all our desires, nor in giving in to all our desires. True freedom comes from the love of God. This is the crucial moment for Elsa in *Frozen*. Her sister, who never stopped loving her and keeps on coming after her, even when she is repeatedly rejected and pushed away, eventually lays down her life for her. And it is that act of selfless, sacrificial love, which melts Elsa's heart and sets her free. She realizes that love is the way to channel her internal desires.

This is a picture of the pathway to freedom. Like Anna, Jesus never stops loving us, and always comes after us, despite our rejection of him and our attempts to push him away. He has laid down his life for us, selflessly and sacrificially, and this sets us free. This act of love liberates us from the sinful nature, because all our sin and shame is destroyed in his death. It also liberates us from the Law because Jesus, in living the perfect life, fulfils the law perfectly. What we couldn't do for ourselves, he has done for us.

We are set free by love, and we are set free to love. These internal desires do not need to be repressed, nor do they need to be indulged; they can be channeled by love. The Holy Spirit sets us free by writing the Law on our hearts and enabling us to do the right thing and want to do the right thing.

The life of freedom is the life of love. The character in *Frozen* who is most free is not Elsa with all her powers, but Anna who is full of love. Freedom is not individual, trying to escape all ties and bonds; it is relational, as we freely love one another. As the British band Mumford & Sons put it, 'Love will not betray you, dismay you, or enslave you/ It will set you free to be more like the man [or woman] you were made to be.'*

The Christian life remains a battle despite this freedom. For to be a Christian means engaging in an external battle against injustice, inequality, poverty, and loneliness. There is a spiritual battle 'against the powers of this dark world and against the spiritual forces of evil in the heavenly realms'.** And there is also an internal battle against selfishness, pride and the desires within that would destroy us and harm other people if we gave into them.

Paul is brutally honest about the struggles he faces. He does all kinds of things he wished he didn't do, and doesn't do lots of things he wished he did do (7:15). But God sets us free, not so that we don't have to fight any battles; he sets us free so that we can fight our battles and win those battles.

Paul confronts us with another a paradox: if you want to be free you need to be slaves of righteousness (6:19). Just as becoming truly alive means dying to ourselves, so true freedom means becoming a slave of God.

When one of our children was three years old, he was afraid of swimming, which is a real disadvantage if you live by the sea. He wouldn't even dip his toes in the water. One day I thought I would try to help him overcome this fear, so I took hold of him and started carrying him towards the water. As I did so I could feel him

---

* Mumford & Sons, 'Sigh No More', *Sigh No More*, Glassnote, 2009.
** Ephesians 6:12.

gripping on to me more and more tightly with his arms and legs.

As I entered the sea with him, Tara was watching from the beach and could hear the screaming that was coming from our son. She was worried that I was causing him some serious trauma, but then she began to realize that they were not screams of terror but screams of delight. He loved it, and I had never seen him enjoy himself so much.

He was free from his fears at last. But he was free because he was holding on to me so tightly. He was free because he was attached to me, and he believed that I was stronger than the water and the waves. As long as he was connected to me, he was free from his fears. He wasn't free from me (he had latched onto me with all his strength), but because he wasn't free from me, he was free from everything else.

This is the true freedom that comes from being loved by God. If you want to be free from God then you'll find yourself enslaved to almost everything else, but if you decide that you want to make God your master, to attach yourself to him totally, you will find yourself totally, joyfully and eternally free.

Chapter 11

SECURITY

The Spirit you received does not make you slaves, so that you live in fear again; rather, the Spirit you received brought about your adoption to sonship. And by him we cry, 'Abba, Father.' The Spirit himself testifies with our spirit that we are God's children. Now if we are children, then we are heirs – heirs of God and co-heirs with Christ, if indeed we share in his sufferings in order that we may also share in his glory.

ROMANS 8:15–17

'A great man doesn't seek to lead. He's called to it. But if your answer is "no", you'd still be the only thing I ever needed you to be: my son.'*

DUKE LETO

I think our insecurities (or at least mine) tend to fall into four categories. First, we can feel insecure about ourselves (our identity, our value, our abilities, our looks, our successes or failures). Second, we feel insecure about our relationships, whether we belong, or are liked or fit in. Third, we feel insecure about the world, which can feel like a frightening place full of threats and dangers. And fourth, we can feel insecure about the future, and what's going to happen to us.

Each of these insecurities is rooted in fear. There is the fear of not being enough – not beautiful enough, not talented enough, not successful enough. There is the fear of being alone or of being rejected. There is a fear of the world around us, and how it might harm us. And there is a fear of the future, and what it holds for us.

* *Dune*, directed by Denis Villeneuve, Warner Bros., 2021.

If we live out of fear things start to go wrong. If we are insecure about our identity, we might pretend to be something we are not, or become critical of other people to try to help us feel better about ourselves. If we are insecure about our relationships, we tend to either keep people at a distance or cling to them. If we feel insecure about the world, we can become controlling, in the attempt to make our environment less of a threat, or passive, avoiding anything that might harm us. And if we feel insecure about the future, we can struggle to make decisions or worry about things that may or may not ever happen.

However, in Romans 8, Paul writes that we are not slaves to fear, but we are children of God. In this section of Romans, described by some as the greatest part of the Bible, we see how the love of God is the answer to every kind of insecurity. We may look for job security or relationship security or financial security, but the most secure people in this world are not the people who are the most beautiful, the most talented, the most successful, not the people with the most friends, or the people with the most comfortable lifestyle, or the people with the most promising prospects. The most secure people are the ones who know that they are deeply loved.

Paul describes our relationship with God as something that gives us total security. He says that 'by [the Spirit], we cry "Abba, Father"' (8:15). 'Abba' was the word used by young children of their father. It is the most intimate, informal way of addressing your father. And it says, 'we *cry* "Abba, Father".' The word for 'cry' is one that suggests deep anguish, like that of a baby crying. Psychologists recognize the importance of crying for a baby's development, because through crying they begin to understand their own needs and desires, and when a parent hears their crying, the parent picks them up and holds them, this communicates to that child that what they need and what they want are important and valuable.

God is this kind of Father. Again and again, the Psalms speak of a God who hears our cries.* He hears your cries of pain and

---

* See Psalm 145:19.

anguish, he knows your deepest needs and desires, and he responds to meet them.

This relationship is both objective and subjective. It is objective in the sense that it is not dependent on our emotional state, whether you feel like you are loved by God. Paul uses the language of adoption, which in the Roman world meant a legal arrangement in which a Roman family would choose someone to adopt and then bring that person into the family on equal status with the other children. It was legal, objective and permanent. Your relationship with God is not dependent on how close to him you feel. It is an objective, permanent reality. However, it is also something subjective, in that it can be experienced, for the Holy Spirit 'testifies with our spirit that we are God's children' (8:16). You can feel it.

SECURE IDENTITY

Firstly, this relationship secures our identity, for we are children of God. Paul says now there is 'no condemnation for those who are in Christ Jesus' (8:1).

The insecurities we feel about our identities lead us into two errors, each of which are equally dangerous: pride and shame. Pride is thinking you are better than other people; shame is thinking you are worse. Pride is thinking you are more important; shame is thinking you are less important. Pride is believing you are good; shame is believing you are all bad. Pride is the denial that you have done anything wrong; shame is feeling that you are wrong. Pride is not being able to admit your mistakes; shame is not being able to escape your mistakes. Pride leads to boasting; shame leads to hiding.

Instinctively we recognize both pride and shame as problems, but try to fix pride with shame, or shame with pride. If someone is feeling ashamed, we might find ourselves telling them 'you've done nothing wrong' to try to build them up. And if we feel someone is full of pride, refusing to admit their own faults, we can find ourselves trying to shame them. But you cannot solve shame with pride, or pride with shame. Only love can rescue us from shame and pride.

God breaks through the dynamics of pride and shame, by securing us with his love. You do not need to see yourself as either good or bad, but primarily as one who is loved. Your identity is no longer characterized by shame or pride, but by forgiveness. You do not need to boast about your faults or hide from them but can confess them confident of God's love.

SECURE RELATIONSHIPS

Secondly, we are secure in our relationships, for the love that God has for us enables us to build other healthy relationships.

In their earliest years children often experience 'separation anxiety', where they fear being separated from their parents, and so cling to them and don't interact with other children or adults. However, as the child grows in confidence that their parents love them and are not going to leave them, they can overcome this separation anxiety. Whatever we experienced as children, Paul insists that nothing can separate us from the love of God.

> *For I am convinced that neither death nor life, neither angels nor demons, neither the present nor the future, nor any powers, neither height nor depth, nor anything else in all creation, will be able to separate us from the love of God that is in Christ Jesus our Lord.*

ROMANS 8:38-39

You need not have any separation anxiety, for your relationship with God the Father is rock solid. You do not need to cling to others in unhealthy ways, nor do you need to hold back out of fear of rejection, you can relate in total confidence as one who is loved.

SECURE IN THE WORLD

Thirdly, we are secure in our relationship with the world. God's love for us gives us confidence in the way that we see the world. Human beings seem to simultaneously crave both security and adventure, and we can find ourselves caught in this tension. However, the love of God fulfils both these desires, giving us the security to embrace an adventurous life. For Paul writes, 'we are more than conquerors through him who loved us' (8:37). God's love gives you all the resources to face the world with confidence.

God may lead you into places that feel insecure, but he does this only to establish a deeper security within you. God may sometimes shake you in order that you might know your true foundation. His love allows you to approach the adventures that this world brings with total security.

SECURE FUTURE

Finally, we are secure in relationship to the future. Our future prospects so often depend on how we are brought up by our parents. The way that we were loved (or not loved) as children often has a huge bearing on our future. But this is the not the only force shaping our future. There is something even more powerful than the love our parents have had for us. Some of us will have had good parents; some will have had bad parents. We may have had absent parents or have lost parents. All of us have had imperfect parents. However, all of us can experience the perfect love of the perfect Father who shapes our future.

All parents pass on faults and issues to their children (though they pass on many good things too). But whatever you've experienced from your own parents there is a greater reality, which is the love of your heavenly Father. You are not limited by your parents' successes, nor are you destined to repeat their failures.

You are not your father; you are not your mother, for you have a Heavenly Father and he is the one who will define your destiny.

Paul writes that in all things God 'works for the good of those who love him' (8:28). He is at work in the good things and the bad things. He is at work in the good things that have happened to you and the good things you've done. He also is at work in the bad things that have happened to you and the bad things you've done. You can be secure knowing that whatever you face, whether it is good or bad, God can turn everything for good. And so, your future is secure.

God's love makes us secure in our identity, our relationships, as we face the world, and face the future. However, we will often *feel* insecure, because we all have strengths and weaknesses, other people will let us down, the world is sometimes a tragically dangerous place, and the future is frustratingly uncertain. But we can be secure even when aware of our insecurities. Paul is just as open about his insecurities in Romans 7 (when he speaks about his struggles with his desires) as he is confident in God's love in Romans 8.

Throughout this part of his letter, Paul repeats the phrase 'we know', but then right at the end when he speaks about the security we can have in the love of God he says 'I am convinced' (8:38). This word could be translated 'I am persuaded'. It suggests that this is something that Paul has come to understand through everything that he has experienced in his life. In all the challenges and difficulties he's gone through, he has experienced God's love in such a way that now he is totally convinced that nothing will ever be able to keep him from this love.

There are many things in the Christian life that we don't know, and we shouldn't pretend that we do. But there are some other things that we do know, and we shouldn't pretend we don't. One thing that you can know is that God loves you, and that love makes you totally secure, and there is nothing in all the world that 'will be able to separate us from the love of God that is in Christ Jesus our Lord' (8:39).

Chapter 12

COMPLETE

And we know that in all things God works for the good of those who love him, who have been called according to his purpose. For those God foreknew he also predestined to be conformed to the image of his Son, that he might be the firstborn among many brothers and sisters. And those he predestined, he also called; those he called, he also justified; those he justified, he also glorified.

ROMANS 8:28–30

'The cross and resurrection are the perfect triumph of the perfect sacrifice of perfect love.'*

WILLIAM TEMPLE

'You complete me.'**

JERRY MAGUIRE

God loves you in all things, in all ways, and for all times.

Everyone wants to be loved. But more than that, we want to be loved *completely*. For some reason it is not enough to be loved partially, or moderately, or temporarily. If someone says to us, 'I love you ... a bit', or 'I love you, when you're not grumpy', or 'I love your sense of humour, but nothing else about you', it doesn't usually make us feel good. It is not enough. We desire to be loved totally, completely and unconditionally.

---

* William Temple, *Christus Veritas*, Macmillan and Company, 1925, p270.
** *Jerry Maguire*, directed by Cameron Crowe, TriStar Pictures, 1996.

And we want to be loved forever. The great romantic films rarely contain lines like, 'I promise I will love you for at least the next five years, maybe even ten, but after that who knows?' Instinctively, we know that it's not enough to be loved now, or even to know that we'll be loved tomorrow. Something within us needs a guarantee that we will be loved forever.

We want to be loved completely and eternally, and yet if we are honest with ourselves we know that we are incapable of loving other people perfectly or forever. I love each of our children and often feel that there is nothing I wouldn't do for them, but when one of our children was just seven weeks old she caught a cold and couldn't breathe through her nose. Apparently one solution for a newborn baby's blocked nose is put your mouth over their nose and suck out their snot. When I heard this suggestion, I quickly realized that there were limits to my love, and we managed to get hold of some nasal drops instead.

We are incapable of perfect love, and we are incapable of eternal love. In *The English Patient*, Katherine Clifton, as she lies injured in a cave in the desert, says to her lover Count Ladislaus de Almásy, 'Promise me you'll never leave me. Promise me you'll always love me.' And he replies, 'I promise I'll never leave you. I promise I'll always love you.' But then he does leave her to try to get help and when he returns she's dead. He was willing to do anything for her, but he couldn't deliver on this promise to love her always and be with her always.*

Some of us hope we will find completion in romantic love, through finding a 'soulmate' who will love us perfectly, understand us totally, and who 'completes' us. But this is impossible. Despite the great joys to be found in romantic love, no other person can love us perfectly and completely. No other person can complete us.

* *The English Patient*, directed by Anthony Minghella, Miramax, 1997.

There is only one source of perfect and eternal love: God himself. And we crave this love because we were made for the God who alone loves us perfectly and eternally. Only God and his love for us can complete us.

A relationship won't complete you. A baby won't complete you. A new house won't complete you. A new job won't complete you. Success or fame or money will not complete you. The only thing that can complete you is a God who loves you completely.

IN ALL THINGS

God loves you *in all things*, for 'we know that in all things God works for the good of those who love him' (8:28). He is at work in ways that you can see and in ways you can't see, in ways you understand and in ways you don't understand.

The Horse and his Boy (the third of C.S. Lewis' *Chronicles of Narnia*) tells the story of Shasta, an orphan who escapes from the cruel and uncaring fisherman who has been his adoptive father since he was a baby. He meets up with a girl called Aravis, who is escaping an arranged marriage, and the two of them find themselves fleeing from lions on several occasions. Near the end of the book Shasta is riding a horse on a mountain path in thick fog when he senses a creature walking next him. Initially afraid, he then starts telling the creature all the terrible things that he has faced in his life and how unfortunate he has been.

'I do not call you unfortunate,' said the Large Voice.

'Don't you think it was bad luck to meet so many lions?' said Shasta.

'There was only one lion,' said the Voice.

'What on earth do you mean? I've just told you there were at least two lions the first night, and – '

'There was only one, but he was swift of foot.'

'How do you know?'

'I was the lion.'

And as Shasta gaped with open mouth and said nothing, the Voice continued. 'I was the lion who forced you to join with Aravis. I was the cat who comforted you among the houses of the dead. I was the lion who drove the jackals from you as you slept. I was the lion who gave the Horses the new strength of fear for the last mile so that you should reach King Lune in time. And I was the lion you do not remember who pushed the boat in which you lay, a child near death, so that it came to shore where a man sat, wakeful at midnight, to receive you.'*

God's love is at work in all kinds of ways that we cannot remember, do not see, and won't understand. This is a love that works in all things and explains all things.

Scientists have searched for a 'Theory of Everything', a single scientific framework that fully explains and links together all physical aspects of the universe. But here we read of the true 'Theory of Everything' – the love of God at work in all things and through all things.

IN ALL WAYS

God's love is not one dimensional. God loves us *in all ways*.

I think a healthy relationship, whether it is friendship, or marriage, or within a family, requires you to able to answer 'yes' to these five questions: do you feel understood by this person? Is this relationship going somewhere? Are you both being intentional (rather than one party being completely passive)? Do you feel affirmed by the other person? Does the relationship bring out the best in you?

* C.S. Lewis, *A Horse and His Boy*, HarperCollins, 2014, pp175–176.

I suppose we are all looking for these things in our relationships: to be known, a sense of purpose, to be chosen, to be affirmed, and to become the best version of ourselves.

The implication of these verses is that God's love fulfils each of these desires.

Being Known

God 'foreknew' us (8:29), which means that he has always known us. God knows us completely and loves us totally.

We long to be known, to be understood, for people to 'get us'. But we also fear that if we are truly known we will not be loved. 'I just want you to know who I am', sang the Goo Goo Dolls in 1998.* Three thousand years before this, David wrote in the Psalms, 'You have searched me, and you *know* me.'** God knows you completely and loves you completely.

Having Purpose

God loves you with a purpose, for 'those he foreknew he also *predestined*' (8:29). You have a destiny, a direction. This is relationship which is literally going somewhere: eternity.

You may be in decline physically, mentally, or professionally, but the love of God means that the best years are always still to come. This relationship will not drift or get stuck or stagnate; it will get better and better. For he has predestined you.

Being Chosen

God's love means that you are chosen, 'for those he predestined he also *called*' (8:30). God decided, 'I want you. I choose you.' To your parents you may have been an accident, a surprise or even a mistake. But for God you were not 'unplanned'; you were not unwanted. You may have experienced rejection throughout your life. You may have been the last to be chosen in team games at school, or repeatedly

* Goo Goo Dolls, 'Iris', *Silver Screen Classics*, 2015.
** Psalm 139:1.

passed over for promotion at work, or pushed away by someone you love, but there is a God who sees you, wants you, and who chooses you.

Being Affirmed

God's love means that you are affirmed, for 'those he called he also *justified*' (8:30). One implication of justification is that now God declares publicly over us that we are forgiven, accepted and that he is pleased with us. As a result of the cross, God chooses to forget our faults and to move on from our mistakes, and instead to speak words of love over us.

We all long for approval and affirmation, and God looks at you and says to you, 'You are my son, you are my daughter. I love you and I'm pleased with you.' You may have had all kinds of terrible things spoken over you in your life. People may have criticized you and verbally abused you, but there is one who thinks that you are amazing, who is your biggest fan and greatest admirer, and he is the only one whose opinion really counts.

Becoming More

God's love means that you can be the best version of yourself, for 'those he justified, he also *glorified*' (8:30). This word 'glorified' refers to the finished work of transformation by the Holy Spirit. When you become a Christian, the Holy Spirit comes to live within you and begins to transform you. This is a love that makes us 'more' not 'less'. We become kinder, braver, more compassionate through this relationship.

Becoming like Jesus doesn't make us less ourselves; it makes us more ourselves. You may feel a pressure to be something you're not, or that you have always had to pretend, but here is a God whose love enables you to be the person you were always meant to be. Some relationships may make us feel less ourselves. This one makes us more ourselves. It's a love that brings out all that is best, kindest, wisest, funniest, and most beautiful within each of us.

God's love is perfect and complete, and we know this because on the cross Jesus experienced the shadow side of this love. On the cross the all-knowing one was misunderstood, the eternal one was finished, the chosen one was rejected, the one most deserving of praise and affirmation was mocked and ridiculed, and the glorious one was beaten and disfigured, stripped and hung on a cross in great shame. All because he completely loves you.

FOR ALL TIMES

He loves you in all things. He loves you in all ways. And he loves you for all times.

God alone is the answer to our longing to be loved for all time. 'Foreknew' refers to the beginning of all things; 'glorified' refers to the end of all things. From start to finish God loves you.

God is the only one who can truthfully say to us, 'I promise I'll never leave you. I promise I'll always love you.' This is the only relationship that will last forever, and the only way that we can truly get a 'happily ever after'.

Only this love will complete you. Success will not complete you. Work will not complete you. Popularity and fame will not complete you. Even the imperfect love of another human being will not complete you. Only the perfect love of the perfect God can complete you. For God loves you in all things, in all ways and for all times. God loves you completely and his love completes you.

Chapter 13

EVERYTHING

*If you declare with your mouth, 'Jesus is Lord,' and believe in
your heart that God raised him from the dead, you will be saved.*
ROMANS 10:9

'You are my greatest adventure. And I almost missed it.'*
MR INCREDIBLE

God's love for us is perfect and eternal. It fills us with peace, joy,
hope, security, freedom, life. Its consequences are endless. Its effect
on our lives is total. This is all we've ever needed. This is all we've
ever wanted. And it will last forever. We can know this love is
real because of the cross. We can experience this love for yourself
through the Holy Spirit.

However, this raises a problem. What if this is not your
experience right now? If God loves you, wouldn't he want
everything to go well in your life? But what if it's not?

Paul confidently asserts,

> *For I am convinced that neither death nor life, neither angels nor
> demons, neither the present or the future, nor any powers, neither
> height nor depth, nor anything else in all creation, will be able to
> separate us from the love of God that is in Christ Jesus our Lord.*

ROMANS 8:38-39

This sounds wonderful, but what do we do when it feels like we *are*
separated from God, or that he seems to be unjust or unfair, when

---

The Incredibles, directed by Brad Bird, Walt Disney Pictures, 2004.

life is confusing and when it looks like God has failed? What should we do when life is turning out very differently to what we'd thought a loving God would do or should do?

I've had a few problems with my back through the years. On one occasion when I visited a back specialist, who immediately worked out the problem. Then he set about fixing the problem. After about five sessions he told me that he had finished his work and my back was now fine. This was great news. The only problem was that my back hurt just as much as before.

The Christian life can sometimes feel like this. We've been told that we're fixed, but we still feel broken. What do we do then? Does this mean that God has failed? Does this mean that God's love isn't real or doesn't work?

These are the questions that Paul addresses in the central section of his letter, for these were the very questions that Paul faced for himself. He had grown up as a faithful Jew and had encountered Jesus whom he recognized as the Jewish Messiah. He knew that Jesus was the fulfilment, not only of his personal longings, but also all the hopes of Judaism. However, for the most part, his own people, his friends and his family had not believed in Jesus. They had not only rejected the Gospel but also rejected Paul, who had been beaten, stoned and imprisoned. And so, he was faced with the question of whether God had failed. He had to work out how to deal with the tension between the love of God, about which he was so confident, and the reality that he was facing, which looked so different.

This is something that all of us face at some point in our life. In these moments you can opt out, deciding that Christianity doesn't work as well as you'd thought it would. Or you can pretend there isn't a tension, that everything is great, even when it isn't. Or you can hold on to God's love, despite the pain and the confusion. If you can do this something greater begins to emerge. For as Paul honestly explores the disappointment, confusion and heartache that he is going through, a new word comes to the forefront of his message.

Up until this point in his letter, Paul has been using a number of words to describe the consequences of what God has done for us: we are 'justified' (made right with God), we have 'peace' (reconciled to God), we have 'joy', 'hope', 'life'. Now, in the middle of his letter to the Romans, the dominant word becomes 'salvation' or 'saved'.

This word 'save' occurs twelve times in Romans, but eight of them are in this section. Salvation means the comprehensive putting right of all things. It means healing, redemption, freedom, becoming whole. It means being rescued from everything that enslaves us and destroys us. It means the total transformation of every part of our lives: our bodies, minds, hearts, desires, relationships, work and rest. And salvation comes from the love of God which changes everything.

God loves you and so wants everything for you. He desires your salvation. And this salvation comes to us through the pain, confusion and disappointment. If we find it hard to grasp this, there are three things that I have found have enabled me to hold on to God's love, when life is difficult and I don't understand what's going on. I try to remember the story, return to simplicity and respond with integrity.

REMEMBER THE STORY

Firstly, we need to remember that we are part of a story. God's love is not an abstract concept, nor is it an impersonal force; it is something we experience in the story of our lives. God loves us as part of his relationship with humanity, which takes place in history.

Throughout his letter to the Romans, Paul has been retelling the story of Israel, going back to Abraham and Isaac, and here Paul is reminding his readers that they are part of a story *which is not yet finished*. The answer to the question of why things haven't turned out as we'd hoped, is that it's not the end of the story. We are in the middle of a story which is wider, deeper and more mysterious than we thought. Salvation is something that we are only beginning to experience and will be complete in the future.

Paul wants his readers to know that the rejection of Jesus by most of the Jewish people is not an accident or a failure, but part of God's purposes, for it has caused the message of Jesus Christ to go to the Gentiles (the non-Jewish people) and that this will one day cause a large number of Jewish people to turn to Jesus. So, what looked like a mistake or a failure, is actually a way of drawing more people into the family of God. The story is just bigger than they had thought, and it is not finished.

Whatever you are going through, whether life has turned out as you expected or not, it is vital we know that the story is always bigger than you think, and it is not finished. For God's love never fails, and he never gives up on you.

Christianity is not just a philosophy we believe or a community we join, it is also a story we enter into. And it's a story in which neither you nor I am the main character. The centre of the story is Jesus Christ. Paul says that 'Christ is the culmination of the law so that there may be righteousness for everyone who believes' (10:4). The word, *telos* which he uses here, means 'end, goal, climax'. Jesus is the climax of the story of Judaism, and the climax of all our personal stories.

Whatever you feel your life has been about, Jesus is the one who makes sense of your story. If it has been about a search for freedom, then know that Jesus is the one who sets you free. If it has been about a search for peace, then know that he is the one who fulfils your search for peace. If it has been a lifelong search to find belonging, then know that he is the one who welcomes you home. Jesus completes all our stories.

The greatest adventure of our lives is found in a person. As Mr Incredible says to Elastagirl in Pixar's *The Incredibles*, 'You are my greatest adventure. And I almost missed it." Jesus is our greatest adventure. You are part of a story that is bigger than you think, and it is not yet finished.

RETURN TO SIMPLICITY

Secondly, we need to return to simplicity.

This story, which we are invited to be part of, is both frustratingly complicated and perfectly simple. This section is perhaps the most difficult part of the whole letter. The language is complicated, in that it is not always certain what Paul means by the words he uses. It is philosophically complicated, because Paul is talking about the tension between human responsibility and God's sovereignty. It is socially and politically complicated, because it concerns the relationship between Jews and Gentiles in Rome in the first century (who hated one another) and the future of God's purposes for Israel, which remains controversial today. And it's also personally complicated because Paul is dealing with things which cause him deep emotional pain.

Yet right in the middle of this complex discussion there is a moment of beautiful simplicity. Paul quotes Deuteronomy 30, where Moses tells the people of Israel that the Law they have received is not impossible to grasp (10:6–8). It has come close to them, so that they do not need to ascend to heaven or descend to the depths to understand it. We do not need to 'ascend into heaven' (trying to know everything or have some mystical experience), nor do we need to 'descend to the depths' (sort out our deepest issues or problems first).

Paul is saying that, in the same way, Jesus has come close to us and made himself available to us, and so it doesn't need to be complicated. Paul says that it is simple: 'if you declare with your

---

* *The Incredibles*, 2004.

mouth, "Jesus is Lord," and believe in your heart that God raised him from the dead, you will be saved' (10:9). It doesn't matter who you are, what your background is, what your religion has been, 'everyone who calls on the name of the Lord will be saved' (10:13).

Every relationship has its complications, because relationships bring together different people, with different personalities, cultures, values and desires. But love has the power to overcome complexity. We see this in the great romantic stories and films, which almost always seem to fit into the same pattern: Two people fall in love, or have the potential to fall in love, but there is something, or some things, which make the relationship complicated (they have markedly different personalities, there are situations beyond their control, one of them happens to be the Prime Minister or they don't speak the same language, for example) and the climax of the story comes when their love for each other overcomes the complexity with a moment of simplicity.

In the 1999 film *Notting Hill*, Hugh Grant (playing a penniless bookshop owner) explains to Julia Roberts (playing the most famous actress in the world) why they cannot be together, laying out all the complications that are keeping them apart. He says to her, 'There are too many films. Too many pictures ... I live in Notting Hill; you live in Beverly Hills. Everyone knows who you are; my mother has trouble remembering my name.' He is saying that it's all too complicated.

But Julia Roberts replies, 'Fine, fine. Good decision ... You know this fame thing, it isn't real. And don't forget that I'm just a girl, standing in front of a boy, asking him to love her.'* She appeals to a love which can overcome the complexity, turning it into something very simple.

Sometimes our relationship with God can get confused and complicated when it's supposed to be simple. Despite the infinite complexities within Christianity, at its heart it is about a God who

---

* *Notting Hill*, directed by Roger Michell, Universal Pictures, 1999.

stands before you and says, 'I love you and I want you to love me.'

Karl Barth, possibly the greatest theologian of the twentieth century, when asked what the most profound theological truth he had ever learned was, replied, 'Jesus loves me, this I know, because the Bible tells me so.'*

In the most difficult times in my life, when everything has become complicated and confusing, there have often been moments of total clarity where everything has been simplified to a single truth: 'I am loved by God.'

RESPOND WITH INTEGRITY

Thirdly, we need to respond with integrity.

We can make things more complex than they need to be by driving a wedge between our private and public lives. We are one thing in private and another in public. This is a loss of integrity, which is the state of being whole, undivided, in harmony with ourselves.

When life is tough it is easy to lose our integrity. The outward expression disappears as we retreat into ourselves. Or the outward expression remains, but internally we have ceased to really believe. But this is exactly the time we need to respond with integrity, with our whole selves.

On the cross Jesus experienced rejection, disappointment, confusion. He felt abandoned by his Father. And yet he gave himself completely because he loved his Father, and he loved us and wanted to make everything right with us. And this total love for us invites us to love him back totally.

In one of the great American teenage dramas of the noughties, *The O.C.*, the geeky Seth Cohen starts dating the beautiful Summer Roberts, but their relationship is kept secret because she is

---

* Karl Barth, quoted in *Karl Barth: Theologian of Christian Witness*, Joseph L. Mangina, Routledge, 2017.

embarrassed by it. He is happy with this arrangement for a while but eventually says to her, 'Look, this whole separation of the public and private sphere isn't working for me anymore. I can't do it. If you won't acknowledge me publicly, I can't acknowledge you privately.' He then gets up on top of the coffee cart in front of his whole school and says to her, 'Acknowledge me now or lose me forever.'*

Paul writes, 'If you confess with your mouth that "Jesus is Lord" and believe in your heart that God raised him from the dead and then you will be saved' (10:9). It is not enough to have an outward expression of faith; there also needs to be an inward commitment. It is not enough to have an inward commitment of faith; we also need an outward expression, for, as Barth insisted, 'faith that believes in God the Father, the Son and the Holy Spirit cannot refuse to become public.'** This is integrity, where there is consistency between the internal and external, the private and the public, what we believe and what we say, where we respond to the one who loves us totally by responding totally.

In tough times, when things don't make sense, and God feels absent, this is precisely the time to give ourselves totally to God. For the total love of God longs for a total response from us.

If you are feeling disappointed, confused or it feels like God is absent, know that the story is not yet finished, that within the complexity is a beautiful simplicity, and do not hold back from giving God everything, for whoever confesses with their mouth and believes with their hearts will be saved.

I wonder whether our love for God is most beautiful and most pleasing to God when it's most illogical for us. In those times where it feels like God isn't listening, when it feels like our desires and our longings aren't important to God, when we are the worst version of ourselves rather than the best, when it feels like we need to hold on

* *The O.C.*, Series One, Episode 20, directed by Josh Schwartz, Fox, 2003.
** Karl Barth, *Dogmatics in Outline*, SCM, 2001, p20.

to what we have, otherwise we will lose everything, these are the times when loving God is most powerful and beautiful. That is how God has loved us. On the cross Jesus Christ himself felt distant from his Father, confused and disappointed, crying out, 'My God, my God, why have you forsaken me?' But he still gave himself totally to his Father. We love God by doing the same. When we don't feel loved, when God feels distant, when we feel disappointed by God, this is exactly the moment to give everything to him and love him in return. The one who loves us completely and has given himself to us completely, invites us to love him completely in return.

PART FOUR

Responding to God's Love (2)
ROMANS 12

Chapter 14

RETURNING GOD'S LOVE

Therefore, I urge you, brothers and sisters, in view of God's mercy, to offer your bodies as a living sacrifice, holy and pleasing to God – this is your true and proper worship. Do not conform to the pattern of this world, but be transformed by the renewing of your mind. Then you will be able to test and approve what God's will is – his good, pleasing and perfect will.

ROMANS 12:1–2

'Love desires no recompense other than to be loved in return; and thus God desires nothing in return for his love for us other than our love.'*

HANS URS VON BALTHASAR

If you say to someone, 'I love you', there is really only one thing you want to hear back from them. Responses like, 'Thank you very much' or 'And I like spending time with you too' are (in my experience) not quite enough. The only response you want from someone when you've told them that you love them is for them to say, 'I love you too.'

Our first response to God's love is receive it, to let him love us. Our second response is to love him back.

For the first part of his letter Paul has focussed on what God has done for us and how he has loved us but now, at the start of Romans 12, Paul switches to how we are to love God. When Paul

* Hans Urs von Balthasar, *Love Alone is Credible*, Ignatius Press, 2004, p107.

writes, 'Therefore, I urge you, brothers and sisters, in view of God's mercy, to offer your bodies as a living sacrifice, holy and pleasing to God – this is your true and proper worship' (12:1), he is saying that in view of everything that God has done for us, all the countless mercies and blessings and the way his love has been poured out for us, we are invited to love God in return.

God loves us and longs for us to love him in return. This is the essence of the Christian life: to love God. When Jesus was asked to sum up the entire Old Testament law, he said, '"Love the Lord your God with all your heart and with all your soul and with your strength and with all your mind", and "love your neighbour as yourself."'* According to St Augustine to be a Christian meant only this, 'Love God and do what you want.'

But what does it mean to love God? At the beginning of Romans 12, Paul describes our response to what God has done for us, and these are three ways to love God in return.

GIVING

First, it means giving ourselves to God. Paul writes, 'Therefore, I urge you, brothers and sisters, in view of God's mercy, to *offer your bodies* as a living sacrifice' (12:1). When Paul refers to 'bodies' he means 'your whole selves.' And sacrifice was an image from the ancient world of devoting something completely to God. He is saying that we should offer the whole of our lives, every part of who we are, to God.

This is how God has loved us. In Galatians Paul writes about 'the Son of God, who loved me and gave himself for me.'** God's love for us means that he has given us everything, giving his life as a sacrifice on the cross. And so loving God means loving him in the same way, by giving everything back.

* Luke 10:27.
** Galatians 2:20.

In the Gospels there are many occasions when Jesus asks people to give up everything to follow him.* This can seem frightening or overwhelming, but Jesus is simply asking to be loved. It's like a marriage proposal, where you declare your love for someone and your willingness to give your whole self to them and ask them to give themselves completely to you.

This is also why loving God is connected to joy, for though there is huge joy to be found in being loved, there is even greater joy to be found in loving others and giving to others. Birthday parties when people bring gifts are not sad times. Weddings, where two people give themselves completely to each other, are not unhappy occasions even though people are giving themselves away. When I think of the times in my life when I have felt the deepest joy, they have often been in an environment where people have given everything out of their love for Jesus: Benedictine monasteries, where the monks have given up all possessions, all freedom, sex and marriage and family life, or Jackie Pullinger's organization in Hong Kong, where helpers who have given up everything to serve Jesus there.

C.T. Studd was born into huge privilege. A member of the aristocracy, educated at Eton and then Cambridge. He was a brilliant sportsman and played cricket for England. He was the remaining 'not out' batsman when England lost to Australia in the match that started the Ashes (and his name is on the Ashes urn). But he gave up everything: his wealth, his lifestyle, his circle of friends, to follow Jesus, becoming a missionary, first in China, then India and Africa. And for him it was all worth it. He said, 'If Jesus Christ be God and died for me, then no sacrifice can be too great for me to make for him.'**

What does it mean to offer a sacrifice to God? There were three main types of sacrifice in the Old Testament: sin offerings, burnt

* See Mark 10:21.
** C.T. Studd, quoted in *C.T. Studd: Cricketer and Pioneer*, Norman Grubb, Lutterworth, 2014, p132.

offerings and fellowship offerings. The sin or guilt offering involved offering a lamb which would in some way embody our sin and bring about forgiveness for us. This is probably not the kind of sacrifice that Paul has in mind, because Jesus' death on the cross has brought us forgiveness and removed the need for any more sacrifices of this type. Paul is more likely to be thinking of the burnt offering and fellowship offering. With the burnt offering the worshipper would bring an offering as a gift to God, dividing up the animal and putting it out, part by part, on the altar. It would represent the life of the worshipper, in effect saying to God, 'Every part of my life I give to you.' Then it was all burnt up totally as a gift to God. The fellowship offering was similar, except at the end the lamb or grain would be given back to the worshipper to eat.

So, some sacrifices (like the burnt offering) meant giving everything to God with nothing left at the end; with others (like the fellowship offering) something was devoted to God, but then given back to the worshipper for him or her to enjoy. This seems to be the pattern of the Christian life when we offer our whole lives to God. When we offer to God money, or a relationship, or our ambitions, either God will respond by taking that thing away from us, knowing that it is not the best thing for us. Or God gives it back, transformed into something even greater.

I have a friend who, on three separate occasions, felt God ask him to be willing to give up a romantic relationship that he was holding on to too tightly. The first time he gave up the relationship, it seemed that God took that relationship away. The second time he did the same thing, and again God took the relationship away. The third time he was again willing to give up the relationship, but this time God gave it back to him and the couple are now married. In Old Testament times you knew which type of sacrifice you were doing and whether you would get anything back at all, but for us, we just give ourselves to God, knowing that he will give us what is right for us.

Loving God involves offering our whole lives to him, for loving requires giving and the greatest love requires us to give our whole selves.

CHANGING

The second way we love God is by allowing ourselves to be transformed. Paul writes, 'Do not conform to the pattern of this world but be *transformed* by the renewing of your minds' (12:2). Loving God means being willing to be changed by his love.

Now, this doesn't mean we have to change for God to love us. God loves us unconditionally, and we are supposed to love other people in the same way. However, real love always brings about a change in the other person. To try to love someone and be loved by that person, but make sure that it has no impact on who you are or how you live, is impossible. We cannot be loved and remain the same, and so to refuse to be changed is to refuse to be loved.

The Greek word that Paul uses here for 'being transformed' is *metamorphosis*, which is used in only two other places in the New Testament. One is in the Gospels, at the Transfiguration, where Jesus is transformed in front of three of his disciples, and his face shines like the sun and his clothes become as white as light. He becomes radiant, transfigured, transformed, and at that moment a voice from heaven says, 'This is my Son, whom I love. Listen to him!'* The radiance and the love are connected. For when you are loved, you become radiant.

The other use of this word is in 2 Corinthians, where Paul says, we all 'who with unveiled faces reflect the Lord's glory.'** In the Old Testament Moses wore a veil because he used to talk to God face to face, and as a result his face would shine so much that he

* Mark 9:7.
** 2 Corinthians 3:18.

had to put a veil over his face to protect the other Israelites. Now, Paul says, 'we all, who with unveiled faces reflect the Lord's glory, are being *transformed* into his image with ever-increasing glory.' Transformation means becoming more like Jesus Christ, the most beautiful, the most perfect, the most fulfilled, the most effective, the kindest, the wisest, the most compassionate, the most powerful, the most humble, the most loving person who has ever existed. And in becoming more like Jesus, we become more like the people God intended us to be. We begin to leave behind our old selves, the selfishness and bitterness and pride, and become more like the people God made us to be.

To love God is to allow him to transform you into the most radiant version of yourself. You cannot love and be loved and stay the same, because love is connection and being connected to someone always means that there is an exchange. To resist change is to resist being really loved. Either we can love the world first and be shaped by the world. Or we can love God first and be shaped by God. If we love the world first, we will become dull and imperfect version of ourselves. If we love God first, we will become a radiant and glorious version of ourselves.

God loves us so much that he was willing to be transformed for our sake. 'The Word became flesh and made his dwelling among us' and 'he made himself nothing by taking the very nature of a servant.'* Jesus Christ loved you so much he allowed himself to be beaten and bruised and disfigured on the cross that you might become radiant and glorious and transfigured through his life.

Loving God means letting yourself be transformed by his love.

SUBMITTING

The third way that we love God is through submission. For love always means putting the other first, putting their desires ahead of

* John 1:14, Philippians 2:7.

your own. Paul writes, ' ... then you will be able to test and approve what God's will is – his good, pleasing and perfect will' (12:2). As we give ourselves to God completely, allowing his love to transform us, we will discover what God wants and desire what he wants above what we want.

This starts with listening. The theologian, Paul Tillich, wrote that 'the first duty of love is to listen.'* We start by listening to and understanding the desires of the other person. But it is only really love if, having listened, we put their desires ahead of ours. Love and submission are inseparable. Jesus' greatest act of love for his Father took place after he had prayed, 'yet not my will, but yours be done.'**

God loves us by submitting to us. He listens to us, and puts our will before his, laying down his life for us. And we love God by doing the same: listening to the God who listens to us, submitting ourselves to the God who submits to us.

This creates a beautiful dynamic in our relationship with God. We say to God, 'What do you want?' and he responds, 'What do you want?' Instead of a competition of wills we have a union of wills. When we enter this dynamic, we begin to know God's will for our lives, and approve God's will for us. It won't be a battle with God. It will be a collaboration with God.

And it will lead to much greater things for our lives, for God's will for us is 'perfect' whereas our desires for our lives are always imperfect. In submitting ourselves to God we swap our imperfect desires for his perfect plans for our lives.

This requires all three elements to work together. If you want to know God's will for your life, and if you want God's will to be something that you approve instead of fighting, then you first need to lay down your life, then allow God to transform your mind, and then you will be able to know and delight in God's will for your life.

* Paul Tillich, quoted in *Beyond Maintenance to Mission: A Theology of Congregation*, Craig L. Nessan, Fortress Press, 2010, p15.
** Luke 22:42.

REFLECTING GOD'S LOVE

So loving God means giving yourself to him, being transformed by him and submitting to him. These seem like difficult, almost impossible things to do, and it is striking that Paul believes this is possible. But it is possible because we love God with the love that he gives us. When Paul says that we do this 'in view of God's mercy', he uses the Greek word *dia* which can mean either 'because of' or 'through'. It is not just because God has loved us, but it is through God's love, that we can love him back.

In sports like tennis or cricket, the batter or tennis player can generate pace on the ball either through their own strength, or by using the existing pace on the ball. It is in this second way that it is possible for us to love God. We love God, not through our own effort, but by reflecting his love for us. We give ourselves to the one who gave everything for us, we are transformed by the one who became flesh for our sake, we submit to the one who laid down his life for us.

And crucially we don't do this alone, nor is it possible to do alone. Paul is not writing about an individual response to God, but a community who is learning to love the God who loves them. We can only do this together, as the community that the love of God creates. But to do this we have to deal with the problem of the self.

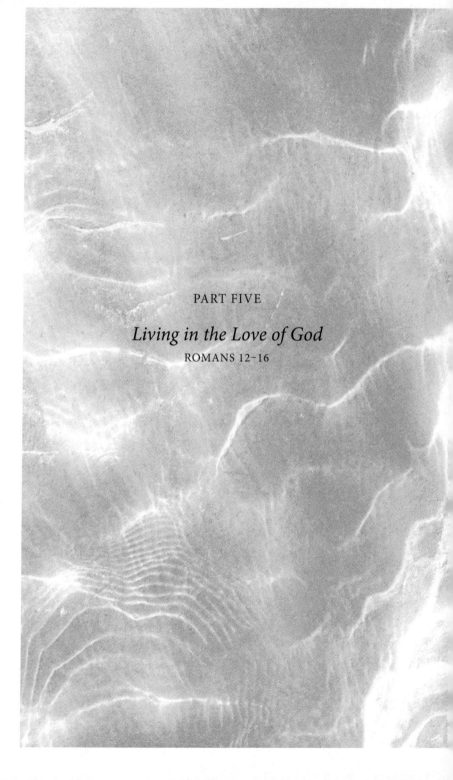

PART FIVE

Living in the Love of God
ROMANS 12–16

Chapter 15

AUTHENTICITY

For by the grace given me I say to every one of you: do not think of yourself more highly than you ought, but rather think of yourself with sober judgment, in accordance with the faith God has distributed to each of you.

ROMANS 12:3

'The greatest of all deceptions is self-deception.'*

PLATO

Being loved by God and loving him in return creates the framework for how we live. It begins to shape how we relate to other people. It redefines our actions and our purpose. It binds us together in a new kind of community. But for it to do all these things, it first of all has to change the way we relate to ourselves. For living in the love of God means embracing authenticity.

There is a gap between the person we are, and the person we wish we were. We struggle to know ourselves, accept ourselves, or to live as our true selves. We see this in the opening chapters of Genesis. Human beings are made good, but by rebelling against God they immediately feel uncomfortable about themselves. They make clothes. They hide. They are disconnected, not only from God and from one another, but also from themselves. As Chesterton put it, 'To the question, "What is meant by the Fall?" I could answer with complete sincerity, "That whatever I am, I am not myself."'**

---

* Plato, quoted in *The Power in Words*, Jeff Cokenour, WestBow Press, 2020.
** G. K. Chesterton, *Orthodoxy*, Hodder and Stoughton, 1999, p236.

And so, we find ourselves searching, not only for God and real community, but also for the person God made us to be. This is the search for authenticity.

DENYING REALITY

One of the challenges with being authentic is that we very often prefer illusions to reality, particularly about ourselves. T.S. Eliot wrote that 'humankind cannot bear very much reality.'* There are some things that are too uncomfortable or painful to face, so we find ourselves trying to deny reality, or escape from reality, or trying to form our own reality. As Iris Murdoch put it, 'We live in a fantasy world, a world of illusion. The great task of life is to find reality.'**

In *Blind Spot: The Hidden Biases of Good People*, Mahzarin R. Banaji and Anthony G. Greenwald describe five different kinds of lies that people tell.*** There are white lies, which are where someone asks us, 'How are you?' and you respond, 'Very well, thank you,' when in fact you are seriously ill. Or when someone asks, 'How do I look?' and you reply, 'You look great,' when they really don't. White lies are an attempt to spare the feelings of another person or hold back unnecessary information that might be a burden to them.

Grey lies are slight modifications of the truth designed to protect yourself. For example, you might send a message to a friend saying, 'I'm on my way,' when you're *about* to be on your way, but haven't yet left the house. Or you might say, 'I'm so sorry I'm late, my train was delayed,' when your train was delayed, but you would have been late anyway because you had left too late.

Red lies are the primal lies we tell to compete in the world, like making up elements of your CV, or pretending you volunteer in an orphanage to impress someone on a date.

* T.S. Eliot, *Four Quartets*, HarperCollins, 2014.
** Iris Murdoch, *The Sea, The Sea*, Random House, 2008.
*** Mahzarin R. Banaji and Anthony G. Greenwald, *Blind Spot: The Hidden Biases of Good People*, Delacorte Press, 2013, pp22–31.

We tell blue lies when we tell people things which are factually false, but we think they express something more generally true about ourselves. For example, if someone asks you whether you voted at the last election, you reply, 'Yes, of course.' Because you are the kind of person who always votes. Admittedly, you forgot to vote at the last election, but you think it would be misleading to say 'no' because you are the kind of person who normally does vote.

All lies create problems, but arguably the most dangerous kind of lie is the fifth kind of lie, which is the colourless lie. These are the lies we tell ourselves. As Fyodor Dostoevsky observed,

> Everyone has reminiscences which he would not tell to everyone but only his friends. He has other matters in his mind which he would not reveal even to his friends, but only to himself, and that in secret. But there are other things that a man is afraid to tell even to himself, and every decent man has a number of such things stored away in his mind.*

We can be afraid to face who we really are, and so tell ourselves that we are better, or kinder, or more loved than we really are.

ESCAPING FROM REALITY

Or we try to escape from reality.

One of the most helpful books I've read on parenting is the highly influential, *How to Talk so that Kids Listen, and Listen so that Kids Talk.*** However, I was struck by one piece of advice in the book, which describes what to do when confronted by the desires of your children that you cannot fulfil. It recommends that you acknowledge their desire ('I can see you really want

* Fyodor Dostoevsky, *Notes from the Underground*, quoted in Banaji and Greenwald, *Blind Spot*, p24.
** Adele Faber, *How to Talk so that Kids Listen, and Listen so that Kids Talk*, Piccadilly Press, 2012.

some chocolate,'), then you recognize the emotion that unfulfilled desire has created in them ('You're feeling sad that you can't have chocolate right now, because it's 3am and we don't have chocolate in the middle of the night'), and finally you give them their desire through fantasy ('Let's imagine that your bed is made of chocolate. Which part of the bed would you eat first?').

Much of this advice seems helpful and healthy, however I wonder how much we attempt to deal with disappointments and the painful reality of our lives with fantasy. When life is painful we escape into the fantasy of films, social media, even televised sport, to avoid the discomfort of our real lives. I know for myself that when I feel hurt or disappointed by something I feel a strong pull into an alternate reality and instinctively look to my phone to follow the news, any sport taking place across the world, social media, work emails, anything to distract me from what I am feeling in that moment.

REFUSING REALITY

One of the most effective ways we begin to understand who we are is through feedback. People tell us that we haven't been doing something as well as we thought, or that we haven't been as kind as we'd imagined. This is not an easy process to go through, and it can be tempting to refuse to accept what is said to us, either by trying to justify or defend ourselves, or by retaliating and pointing out all the faults or weaknesses in the other person. No feedback is ever given perfectly, which means that we can always look to the failings of the method of feedback, its timing, or any elements that weren't fair within it, rather than seeking to embrace anything within it that was accurate.

But refusing feedback is just another way in which we deny the reality of who we are.

FORMING OUR OWN REALITY

Finally, we can try to form our own reality. This is the mantra of 'Be who you want to be.' It is no longer enough to be able to do what we want; we also want to be able to reshape the reality of ourselves. However, when we do this reality tends to hit back. If you're an introvert trying to be an extrovert, sooner or later it will have an impact. One of the reasons I got chronic fatigue while I was at university was that I was trying to live a life that did not match the reality of who I really was. I could try to pretend that I was someone who only needs five hours sleep a night, but in reality I seemed to need more like nine (if not more).

The reason we avoid, or deny, or try to escape from the truth about ourselves is that deep down we don't really believe that we are loved, and so we project an idealized version of ourselves, or try to become a version of ourselves that we think people might love, or just try to avoid thinking too much about who we really are. Or we are so overwhelmed by our weaknesses and failings that we fall into despair, hating ourselves, rather than being our true selves.

However, the love of God enables us to be ourselves, breaking through our pretenses, our falsehoods and our self-deceptions. It gives us the security to recognize who we are and to face reality. It enables us to live authentically.

TRUE AUTHENTICITY

Paul writes, 'For by the grace given me I say to every one of you: do not think of yourself more highly than you ought, but rather think of yourself with sober judgment, in accordance with the faith God has distributed to each of you' (12:3). Eugene Peterson paraphrases this verse in THE MESSAGE, 'The only accurate way to understand ourselves is by what God is and by what he does for us, not by what we are and what we do for him.'

The authentic life – knowing who we are, being truly ourselves, being genuinely authentic – comes from our relationship with God. For this relationship secures us, so that we can face the reality of who we are without the fear of rejection. It confronts us, because the perfect love of God reveals to us our own imperfections. It's not that we admit our faults so that we can be loved; we are loved and so can admit our faults. God's love is precisely what enables us to face these failures and these weaknesses in the knowledge that we are loved. It enables us to see ourselves as we really are. The more we know that we are loved, the more we can own our struggles, and be honest about the things that aren't right within us. And so finally we can be ourselves.

Authenticity is made possible by the love of God, but it is also commanded by God. Paul commands the Church in Rome not to think too highly of themselves, which suggests that he thought of it as a choice. We need to decide to leave behind fantasy and embrace reality, we need to choose to face the truth about ourselves, and start living as ourselves.

To do this we need to follow the only perfect example of true authenticity. The authentic life is revealed to us most clearly in Jesus, who is the one person in history who has been, and is, completely himself. In the Old Testament God reveals his name to Moses as 'I am who I am.' This is a declaration of the unchanging nature of God, the faithfulness of God, the self-existence of God (he doesn't depend on anyone else or anything else for his existence), and also the *authenticity* of God, a God who is truly himself. In the New Testament Jesus adopts this same language for himself. He says to the disciples, 'Take courage. It is I. Don't be afraid'; to the Samaritan woman, 'I who speak to you, I am he'; and to the teachers of the Law, 'Before Abraham was born, I am.'*

* Matthew 14:27, John 4:26, John 8:58.

Jesus is the great I AM, the truly authentic one who shows us what it is to be authentic. And the reason he is able to be himself more than anyone in history, is because he knew that he was loved more than anyone in history. Jesus provides us with the model of how to live authentically, particularly in his modesty, vulnerability and self-sacrifice.

Modesty

Authenticity means modesty, not self-promotion. We do not need to impress anyone, or promote ourselves in any way. In the Gospels there is a theme which theologians call 'the messianic secret'. It refers to all the occasions when, following a healing, someone being raised from the dead, or Jesus shining on the mountainside at the Transfiguration, he tells his disciples, or the recipients of his healing, not to tell anyone. Today in the age of the Instagram post, you would expect something like: 'just raised someone from the dead #new life' or 'transfiguration selfie #no filter #glow' or 'honoured to hang out with @Elijah and @realMoses #legends'. Instead, he says to them, 'tell no one.'

The person who in the history of the world had most to boast about, is the one who boasts least. He doesn't need to promote himself because he knows he's loved.

It is the same for you. God is already pleased with you, he already loves you, and so you do not need to promote yourself to the world. You can be secure in the knowledge that the one who truly matters already loves you.

Vulnerability

Authenticity means vulnerability. There is no need to hide our struggles. When Jesus is raised from the dead, he appears to his sceptical disciples, needing to reassure them that it is really him. The way he proves it really is he himself, is not by performing a miracle, reciting his best sermons or finding some water to walk on. Instead, he demonstrates his authenticity, by showing them his hands and feet, the signs of rejection, pain, humiliation, failure, defeat, and shame. He shows himself to his disciples in vulnerability.

This is what it means to be authentic. Because we are loved we can be vulnerable. We can let people see us at our worst and most broken.

Self-sacrifice

And authenticity means self-sacrifice. Authenticity does not require us to demand our own way. I once asked a friend to help me with something that I was unable to do myself, and he replied, 'No. I don't want to.' I think I looked disappointed, and so he said in his defense, 'I'm just being authentic.' As I walked away, I wondered whether he was right. Maybe he was being authentic to a part of who he was. But this is not true authenticity, which is aligning ourselves with the people that God made us to be. Doing whatever you want isn't being truly authentic; it's being selfish and lacking self-control.

Being selfish is not true authenticity. Authenticity is not about asserting yourself in the world, but giving up your life for the world. Just before he died, Jesus was praying in the garden of Gethsemane, 'Father, if you are willing, take this cup from me; yet not my will, but yours be done.'* He knew who he was: the Son of the Father. He knew what he wanted: to escape death on the cross. But he was able to give up his desires for the sake of the world that he loved. At the moment of Jesus' greatest sacrifice on the cross, the centurion saw how he died and said, 'Surely this man was the Son of God!'** By giving himself up, it became clear who he really was.

BECOMING OURSELVES

We cannot become ourselves by ourselves. Only God can enable us to be truly ourselves, for only he is able to strip away our false

* Luke 22:42.
** Mark 15:39.

selves, the lies we have told ourselves about being better than we are, kinder than we are, more important than we are, and the lies about being worthless, unlovable, without hope. This process of removing the lies to reveal the truth can be an uncomfortable, even a painful experience.

In the fifth of C.S. Lewis' *Chronicles of Narnia*, *The Voyage of the Dawn Treader*, there is a beautiful scene. Eustace, who is a boy from our world and is selfish, arrogant and a pain to everyone, gets turned into a dragon. And then he meets Aslan, who tells him to take off his dragon skin. Eustace scratches at his skin and removes a layer, but he looks down and sees that he's still a dragon. He tries again and again, and each time the same thing happens: he removes a layer of skin, but he remains a dragon. Then Aslan insists that only he can do it. Eustace describes the experience like this:

'The very first tear he made was so deep that I thought it had gone right into my heart. And when he began pulling the skin off, it hurt worse than anything I've ever felt. The only thing that made me able to bear it was just the pleasure of feeling the stuff peel off. You know – if you've ever picked the scab of a sore place. It hurts like billy-oh but it *is* such fun to see it coming away.'

'I know exactly what you mean,' said Edmund.

'Well, he peeled the beastly stuff right off – just as I thought I'd done it myself the other three times, only they hadn't hurt – and there it was lying on the grass: only ever so much thicker, and darker, and more knobbly-looking than the others had been ... Then he caught hold of me ... and threw me into the water. It smarted like anything but only for a moment. After that it became perfectly delicious and as soon as I started swimming and splashing I found that all the pain had gone from my arm. And then I saw why. I'd turned into a boy again."*

* C.S. Lewis, *The Voyage of the Dawn Treader*, HarperCollins, 2014, pp117–118.

The love of God enables you to be yourself, and commands you to be yourself. As St Catherine of Sienna put it, 'Be who God made you to be and you will set the world on fire."*

* Catherine of Sienna, quoted in *Stirring Waters: Feminist Liturgies for Justice*, Diann L. Neu, Liturgical Press, 2020, p31.

Chapter 16

BELONGING

For just as each of us has one body with many members,
and these members do not all have the same function, so in
Christ we, though many, form one body, and each member
belongs to all the others.

ROMANS 12:4–5

'All we have to see/ Is that I don't belong to you/ You don't
belong to me/ Freedom.'*

GEORGE MICHAEL

The cult science fiction series, *Quantum Leap*, which ran from
the late 1980s to the early 1990s, began each episode with this
explanation of the story:

Theorizing that one could time travel within his own lifetime,
Doctor Sam Beckett stepped into the Quantum Leap accelerator
and vanished. He awoke to find himself trapped in the past, facing
mirror images that were not his own, and driven by an unknown
force to change history for the better. His only guide on this journey
is Al, an observer from his own time, who appears in the form of a
hologram that only Sam can see and hear. And so, Doctor Beckett
finds himself leaping from life to life, striving to put right what once
went wrong, and hoping each time that his next leap will be the leap
home ... **

* George Michael, 'Freedom!', *Listen Without Prejudice Vol 1.*, 1990.
** *Quantum Leap*, created by Donald P. Bellisario, NBC, 1989–1993.

In many ways we are all trying to come home. Deep down we feel restless and out of place. We find ourselves leaping from job to job, relationship to relationship, screen to screen, hoping each time that the next leap will be the leap home. I remember watching that final episode of *Quantum Leap* in 1993, which ended with the tragic line, 'Sam Beckett never returned home.' That can be our fear – that we will never really find our home.

This search for home is a search for belonging. Belonging is about being accepted and known. It is having a place. It is the opposite of alienation and isolation. Ultimately, it is about being loved. We don't just want to be admired; we want genuine connection. It is not enough to have fans; we need to have family. We don't just want to be popular; we want to belong. And yet there is something deep within us that often makes us feel that we don't quite belong.

And just as we struggle to know that we ourselves belong, and we are also not always good at helping other people to belong. We find ourselves rejecting, alienating or excluding people, whether consciously or unconsciously.

Ultimately this is a spiritual problem which has existed since the Fall. When sin entered the world, it began to undo the way that human beings were supposed to relate to one another, resulting in blame, hostility, conflict and isolation. And the consequence is a loss of belonging.

AUTHENTICITY AND BELONGING

This desire for belonging is often in conflict with our desire for authenticity. For we want to be truly ourselves and we want to be truly with others. We are looking for both individuality and community, simultaneously wanting to stand out and fit in. We find ourselves sacrificing authenticity to belong or sacrificing belonging to be authentic.

But the love of God is the answer to our longings for both authenticity and belonging, for it is a love that enables us to be our true selves and be truly with others, a love that holds together individuality and community. For we are loved individually, seen and known by God, set free to be ourselves. But we are also loved into a community. God's love connects us, binds us together, without us losing ourselves.

This is how God works in his own nature. God is Father, Son and Holy Spirit, three persons united in perfect love. He is perfectly one, and each person is perfectly themselves. His unity does not compromise each person's authenticity, and the authenticity of the persons does not undermine God's unity.

In this part of the letter, we see belonging and authenticity working together. Paul is using the image of a body, which is an image of connection, in which 'each member belongs to all the others' (12:5).* However, five times Paul addresses 'each of you' (12:3–8). For Paul is describing a kind of community where the individual is not lost for the sake of the whole. It is a community of both authenticity and belonging.

This is the kind of community that Paul is trying to encourage in Rome, and it is the community that each of us is looking for. And to have this kind of real belonging we tend to need four things: humility, permanence, diversity and contribution.

Humility: Seeing yourself as you are

First, we need humility, which enables us to see ourselves as we really are.

The verse we looked at in the previous section, 'Do not think of yourselves more highly than you ought … ' (12:3) is the key, not only for authenticity, but also for belonging. For humility is essential for community. Pride says, 'I don't need anyone else. I'm fine on my

---

* There is no Greek word for 'belong' in this verse (or in 1:6). It literally says that 'each one members of one another'.

own.' But Humility says, 'I need other people. I am not myself by myself.' Humility recognizes I can't do life on my own. I don't know it all; I can't do it all. We are meant to live in community. For we do not hold the whole truth, we do not have a total perspective on our own. And we can't do it all alone.

Humility creates belonging, as we recognize that we are not ourselves without other people. As the journalist, Tobias Jones, put it, 'We are all encrypted and it is other people who introduce us to ourselves by providing the code.'*

Permanence: Being committed beyond convenience

Second, belonging needs permanence, as we commit ourselves to one another beyond what is convenient.

I was at a wedding once where the person praying for the couple prayed that God would '*literally* glue them together', which I don't think she really meant, and thankfully God did not answer. God may not literally glue us together, but he does bind us together into one body, and it is this bond which creates belonging.

Belonging requires permanence. Belonging needs attachment, commitment, knowing that whether I like it or not, I am yours and you are mine. This is one of the key implications of the image of the body that Paul uses for the Christian community. We are necessarily and permanently connected. If we separate, we die.

True belonging comes from commitment, where we know that there is nothing we can do to lose our place in the community. When we are simply fitting in, our place in the group is conditional. If you find yourself at a different stage of life (like remaining single when everyone else gets married), or you express an opinion that no one else shares, or you make a mistake and hurt the people around you, then suddenly you are no longer part of the group. When similarity is lost, so is the community. Our place is always fragile and unstable. And there is no true belonging.

* Tobias Jones, *Dreams of Utopia*, Faber and Faber, 2007, p182.

This is the difference between belonging and fitting in. Community based on agreement is not belonging; it's fitting in. Community based on similarity is not belonging; it's fitting in. Community because you're all at the same stage of life is not belonging; it's fitting in. Fitting in is fragile. Belonging is strong. And it comes from permanence.

Paul has said that nothing can separate us from the love of God – neither height nor depth, neither angels nor demons, neither the present nor the future (8:38–39). This kind of love, which refuses to be separated, then begins to flow through us into our relationships with other people. The permanent love of God begins to enable us to love others permanently.

Each of us will have various relationships of varying quality. We make friends, fall out, make up, drift apart. We have connections of different strengths with different people. Some of these relationships may be incredibly strong and beautiful, some might be strained and awkward. There are others with whom we seem to have nothing in common.

But when we are joined to Jesus Christ, we start to experience this love which is total, unconditional, committed and permanent. This is a relationship which is on a different level to even the best of our human relationships. And then this attachment begins to enable us to attach ourselves to the people around us, to those we might find difficult, to those where there is no other common ground.

Paul writes here that we belong to each other, but he has already written, right at the start of his letter, that we 'belong to Jesus Christ' (1:6). We belong to Jesus, and so we belong to each other. When we are attached to Jesus, we become attached to one another. Our relationships will remain imperfect, and sometimes they will be difficult and painful, but an unbreakable bond has been created between us with the power to transform all our relationships.

The permanent love of God begins to bring permanence to our other relationships, and we begin to belong.

Diversity: Being imaginative in your relationships

Third, belonging requires diversity, as we become imaginative in our relationships.

We naturally avoid diversity, relating most easily to people who look like us, or think like us, or live like us. This is a universal problem, often invisible and unconscious. We all have biases and blind spots and a tendency to cling to the safety of similarity. This can be the cause of all kinds of injustice, but it also destroys our sense of belonging.

In 1968 two of the pioneers of the internet, J.C.R. Licklider and Bob Taylor, wrote a paper with the title, 'The Computer as Communication Device'. In it they predicted that the invention of the internet would open up all kinds of beautiful possibilities and that as a result, 'Life will be happier for the online individual because the people with whom one interacts most strongly will be selected more by commonality of interests and goals than by accidents of proximity.'* In other words, we would no longer need to talk to our neighbours, who are different from us. Instead, we would be set free to interact only with those who have the same interests and opinions as us, even if they live on the other side of the world.

The prediction was true in that we can now much more easily find people with common interests and common ideas. But it does not appear to have made us happier. In fact, the invention of the internet has coincided with higher levels of unhappiness and loneliness. We have a natural tendency to sort ourselves into the social settings we prefer, reading the news that reflect our existing views, reading the books that confirm our opinions, watching content that feeds back to us our own thoughts.

* Walter Issacson, *Innovators*, Simon & Schuster, 2014, p261.

Another prediction that emerged with the invention of the internet was that all opinions would become moderate, because as soon as one person expressed an opinion, they would immediately hear about an alternative opinion on the other side of the argument, and gradually everyone would become more balanced, more moderate, with each person able to see both sides of all arguments. But this prediction failed to appreciate our innate tendency to find people who agree with us and reject people that don't, resulting in opinions becoming more extreme in the age of the internet rather than the reverse.

True belonging requires diversity. A community, like a body, is meant to be made up of different parts. Difference is the key. The belonging you are looking for will be found in people who seem very different to you.

Belonging does not come from friendships only with those who look like you, think like you, or are going through the same things as you. We need to be imaginative in our relationships. For God has been imaginative in his love for us. God has existed from all eternity as Father, Son and Holy Spirit, loving one another in perfect love before all times. But then in his infinite imagination and grace, God made the world, the universe and everything in it, and out of all the planets he had made, he chose ours, and of all the species on this planet he chose human beings, breathing his Spirit into them so that they could love in return. It is extraordinary and surprising that God has chosen to love us, human beings. God does not just love people who are like him, and he expects us to do the same.

This is what the Church was always meant to be, and it is a shameful tragedy when the Church has rejected diversity in favour of similarity. It is the opposite of what the Church was made for. This is still the potential of the Church, for we are bound together by a love that is more powerful than prejudice, ignorance or fear, the love of God which binds us to all Christians everywhere: from Nigeria, to China, to America and to Christians from all times in history: from Mary the mother of Jesus and the Apostle Paul to Alfred the Great and Joan of Arc, and Martin Luther and Mother Teresa to St Augustine of Hippo and Julian of Norwich.

Contribution: Giving away what you have been given

Fourth, belonging requires contribution, as we give away what we have been given.

Belonging is more than being known, accepted and welcomed in. Belonging is having a role to play. We belong when we move from being consumers to contributors. Consumerism is not intrinsically bad. We need to consume food, water, and air, or we die. We also need to be spiritual consumers, for Jesus is the Bread of Life,[*] the central act of worship in the Church is communion, and Jesus said that 'Man shall not live on bread alone, but on every word that comes from the mouth of God.'[**] If we are not consumers spiritually, we are going to be spiritually malnourished. However, belonging takes place when we are both consuming and contributing, giving and receiving, taking in and giving out.

We contribute by giving away what we've been given. Paul writes that 'we have different gifts, according to the *grace* given to each of us' (12:6). What we have is a result of grace, which means it is something given to us. And we are supposed to think of whatever we have (our time, money, skills, experience, possessions) as gifts for the community. Our gifts are not for the sake of our sense of worth, to compete, to stand out, or to be special, but have been given to us for the sake of the community.

Paul lists seven different types of contribution we can make: prophecy, serving, teaching, encouragement, giving, leadership and mercy. These are ways in which we pass on to others whatever God has given to us.

[*] John 6:35.
[**] Matthew 4:4.

If your gift is prophesying, then prophesy in accordance with your faith; if it is serving, then serve; if it is teaching, then teach; if it is to encourage, then give encouragement; if it is giving, then give generously; if it is to lead, do it diligently; if it is to show mercy, do it cheerfully.

ROMANS 12:6–8

Paul seems to be saying, 'Just get on and do it.' Don't wait to be asked. Don't expect credit or thanks or recognition. If God has given you any of these things, just get on and use these gifts for the sake of the community.

These things are given to us through the grace of God. We are simply passing on what we've been given. And everyone can contribute, because everyone is loved by God, and that is something that all of us can pass on. There may be times when you feel you have nothing to offer, when you feel useless, weak, unwanted, or unnoticed, but you are loved by God and so you have something to offer. You are loved and so you belong.

BELONGING AT THE CROSS

In Jesus Christ you belong. Those who felt most excluded, rejected, unwanted and on the edge, found they belonged when they were with Jesus. And through his death on the cross Jesus made belonging possible forever. His death was the opposite of belonging, where he himself was unwanted, rejected, abandoned, and betrayed, but through his death our relationship with God is restored and our relationships with one another are made new.

John's Gospel tells us that just before he died, Jesus looked down from the cross and saw his best friend and his mother. He said to his friend, 'This is your mother' and to his mother, 'This is your son.' And it says that from that moment onwards this disciple took Mary into his home.* On one level Jesus was being a faithful son, ensuring that his mother would be cared for when he was gone. But he was also pointing to a greater significance of what he was achieving on the cross, the creation of a home and a family for everyone. For the cross makes it possible to belong. It has brought us home.

* John 19:26–27.

Chapter 17

TRUE LOVE

*Love must be sincere. Hate what is evil; cling to what is good.
Be devoted to one another in love. Honour one another above
yourselves. Never be lacking in zeal, but keep your spiritual
fervour, serving the Lord. Be joyful in hope, patient in affliction,
faithful in prayer. Share with the Lord's people who are in need.
Practice hospitality.*

*Bless those who persecute you; bless and do not curse. Rejoice
with those who rejoice; mourn with those who mourn. Live in
harmony with one another. Do not be proud, but be willing to
associate with people of low position. Do not be conceited.*

*Do not repay anyone evil for evil. Be careful to do what is right
in the eyes of everyone. If it is possible, as far as it depends on
you, live at peace with everyone. Do not take revenge, my dear
friends, but leave room for God's wrath, for it is written: 'It is
mine to avenge; I will repay,' says the Lord. On the contrary:*

*'If your enemy is hungry, feed him;
if he is thirsty, give him something to drink.
In doing this, you will heap burning coals on his head.'
Do not be overcome by evil, but overcome evil with good.*

ROMANS 12:9–21

"'Love your enemies.' This command is an absolute necessity
for the survival of our civilization. Yes, it is love that will save
our world and our civilization, love even of enemies."

MARTIN LUTHER KING

* Martin Luther King Jr., 'Loving your enemies', 1957.

There were a number of words for 'love' in the ancient world in which Paul lived: *eros*, which referred to romantic love; *philia*, which was used of friendship; and *storge*, which means affection, like the love of parents for their children.* However, the Greek word that Paul uses for the love of God is *agape*. This is something distinct from the natural, human loves of family, friendship, and romance, good though these things are. This is a love that is unconditional and self-sacrificial. It is radical and supernatural. It is a love that goes beyond what we might think is reasonable or sensible. It is undeserved, unexpected, and unlimited.

In the first part of Romans Paul uses *agape* exclusively to describe God's love for us, but now *agape* becomes his way of describing how we are to love other people. The same love that we have experienced from God, the love demonstrated on the cross and poured into our hearts through the Holy Spirit, has become the model for all our relationships. We are to love one another *in the same way* that we have been loved by God.

This has inexhaustible implications for us. In Romans 12:9–12, Paul describes this kind of love for one another, firing off around twenty-four different commands in thirteen verses. But let's focus on three ways that we pass on God's love to one another.

RADICAL AUTHENTICITY

First, we are love one another with a radical authenticity. The same love that enables us to be truly authentic, enables us to love one another authentically. Paul writes, 'Love must be sincere. Hate what is evil; cling to what is good' (12:9).

The love that Paul describes is one without pretense. The word translated 'sincere' is *anhypocrites* which means 'without a mask.'

---

* This is an oversimplification. In ancient Greek the meaning of these words often overlapped and are not easy to distinguish.

Paul is describing a love that doesn't operate on a superficial level, but which sees people for who they are and allows them to see who you are.

I imagine we are all looking for this: for someone to see us as we genuinely are, and to love us all the same. That is what makes marriage both beautiful and courageous, for in marriage you invite someone else into your life where you can't hide. They will see all your flaws, all your weaknesses and yet are committed to loving you just as you are.

And what is true of marriage is supposed to be true of all Christian community. In 2010 the journalist Tobias Jones established a community at Windsor Hall Wood, inviting anyone who wanted to come and stay with him and his wife and their young children. People who were homeless, bereaved, struggling with addictions or relationship breakdowns came to stay, and he wrote *A Place of Refuge* about their experience.

> In a community there is nowhere to hide. A mirror is held right to your face and shows you how irrationally, angrily, impetuously and thoughtlessly you act ... I could be surprisingly patient with other people's faults, but I was fed up with seeing my own so frequently. That was the aspect of hospitality I found hardest: not living with strangers' foibles but being forced to witness my own.[*]

This is the challenge of authentic community. There's no perfect community, no perfect relationship, or family, or friend, or church, so either we can spend our time trying to look for the perfect partner or the perfect group of friends or the perfect workplace, or we can decide to love one another as we are.

This authentic love involves both affirmation and confrontation. We are to both 'cling to what is good' and 'hate what is evil' (12:9). For, to really love anyone or anything means also hating something. If you love justice, you must also hate injustice. If you love unity,

[*] Tobias Jones, *A Place of Refuge*, Quercus, 2015, p57.

you must hate division. If you love compassion, you must also hate hard-heartedness. This is an essential part of loving one another with the radical love of God.

This does not come naturally to many of us. When we're confronted with the imperfections of others, we often either try to ignore them, persuading ourselves they don't matter or don't exist, or we can focus on their faults to such an extent that we stop loving them. Our affection for those we love can cause us to minimize the things they do wrong; or our awareness of the things they do wrong can prevent us from loving them. But authentic love means neither ignoring someone's weaknesses, nor ceasing to love them when you encounter them. For we are to 'hate what is evil', rather than denying it, and we are to cling on to what is good, rather than forgetting it.

Loving one another authentically does not require us to approve of everything that another person does. It can be tempting to believe that if people really loved us, they would approve of our lifestyle and choices. But authentic love is not unconditional approval; it's unconditional love.

I saw this clearly during a party I attended while I was at university. There was someone I knew there who was getting dangerously drunk. He repeatedly attempted to stand on tables and then would fall off, hurting himself. I knew that he had two groups of friends at this party. One group seemed to approve of what was happening, and they were buying him more drinks and laughing as he climbed and fell. The other group of friends, whom he knew from our church, clearly didn't approve of what he was doing. But it was this second group of friends who got him out of the party, into a taxi (which they paid for), took him home, got him into bed, cleared up his vomit when he was sick, got him water and a bucket next to his bed, and made sure he was okay. Now which group of friends really loved him? Was it the group that approved or the group that didn't?

Sometimes we think we are searching for approval when we are searching for something more. We are searching for authentic love. For God's love for you doesn't mean he approves of everything that you do. In fact, it means that he will confront you with the things that aren't right in your life, with perfect timing and perfect patience. He does not cease to love you because of your failures, but neither does he simply ignore them. And he clings on to the good in you even when you've given up on any good in yourself.

RADICAL INCLUSION

Second, we are to love one another with radical inclusion.

Paul writes, 'practice hospitality' (9:13), or more literally, 'pursue hospitality', before going on to describe a love that goes beyond the normal expectations of community. This is a love which enables us to love those who are different from us, at a different life stage, different ethnicity, different values, beliefs, personalities, and interests. This includes a love of enemies, loving those who attack us, loving people who are experiencing things that we are not experiencing (whether joy or grief).

God's love inspires us to reach out, to include and welcome in. However, this is made harder by our own need to be included. We can sometimes be so focused on our efforts to belong, that we forget about those on the edge. C.S. Lewis described this tendency in his article, 'The Inner Ring'.* He writes about how, when you encounter a new environment like a school, a college, a new working environment or a church, you discover that there are people there who already know each other. So, you try to get included in this 'ring' of people. However, if you are successful, you quickly discover that there is an 'inner ring' of people within that group that know each other particularly well and from which you are excluded. If you somehow manage to become part of this ring, you then discover that there is an inner ring within this group too.

* C.S. Lewis, *The Weight of Glory*, Touchstone, 1996, pp107–118.

And so, you can find yourself forever searching for an inner ring that is always elusive.

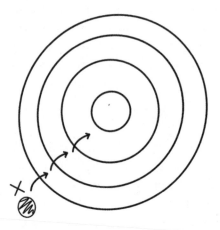

However, right at the centre of the universe there is the true inner ring of God himself, who is Father, Son and Holy Spirit. The reason we are often searching for this 'inner ring' is that we were made for God himself. And when you become a Christian, you're invited into this inner ring. You are brought into the heart of the universe. So, you cannot be more central to things than you are now. You cannot be more at the heart of things if you tried.

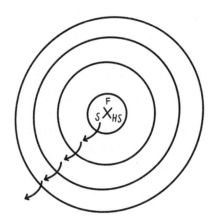

Consequently, instead of searching for your own inclusion, for an 'inner ring' that you will never quite reach, you can focus outwards on including people who are on the edge of your community, and those on the very margins of society. When you enter a room, you can either look for the most important people, or the most attractive people, or the safest people, and gravitate towards them, or you can look around for anyone who might feel like they least belong or are least valuable and move towards them.

This is how Jesus loved people. Jesus was at the very heart of the universe. He knew that he was loved by the Father, and so you never get the impression in the Gospels that Jesus was trying to get invited to the right parties, or be seen with the right people, or involved with the people who make the important decisions. He knew he was loved, and so he went to the margins, to the people who were excluded, whether on the basis of gender, or ethnicity, or illness or their own bad decisions.

No matter how far we flee from God, he brings us from the edge to the centre, and this is how we are to love the world, looking to make sure no one is excluded, no one is left out.

In *The Hiding Place*, Corrie ten Boom tells of her experience sheltering Jews in Holland during the Second World War, and then, having been discovered, attempting to survive, with her sister Betsie, life in a concentration camp, in Ravensbrück, Germany. She describes how, one December day in the camp, as all the prisoners had to stand to attention in the bitter cold, a girl with a learning disability 'suddenly soiled herself. A guard rushed at her, swinging her thick leather crop while the girl shrieked in pain and terror. It was always more terrible when one of these innocent ones was beaten.'

She then whispered to her sister, 'Betsie … what can we do for these people? Afterward, I mean. Can't we make a home for them and care for them and love them?' And Betsie replied, 'Corrie, I pray every day that we will be allowed to do this! To show them that love is greater.'

Then Corrie writes, 'It wasn't until I was gathering twigs later in the morning that I realized that I had been thinking of [the girl who was beaten], and Betsie of their persecutors.'*

RADICAL COMMITMENT

Third, we are to love one another with a radical commitment.

Paul's description of love in these verses involves commands which suggest commitment: 'Be joyful in hope, patient in affliction, faithful in prayer' (12:12), 'be devoted to one another with brotherly love' (12:10). The Greek word he uses for 'be devoted' is *philostorga*, which is a description of parents loving their children. 'Brotherly love' is the word *philadelphia* which is the love of brothers and sisters. The bonds of family are unbreakable and permanent, in that we do not cease to be parents and children, brothers and sisters. Just as nothing can stop God from loving us, and he is totally committed to us, we are to love one another with total commitment.

The American pastor David Wilkerson worked with teenage gangs in New York in the 1950s. In his classic book, *The Cross and the Switchblade,* he describes the moment when he met a gang member called Nicky Cruz. He said that Nicky (who later became a Christian and one of the leaders of Teen Challenge) was the hardest person he'd ever come across:

'How do you do, Nicky,' I said.

He left me standing with my hand outstretched. He wouldn't even look at me …

'Go to hell, Preacher,' he said …

'You don't think much of me Nicky,' I said, 'but I feel differently about you. I love you, Nicky.' I took a step towards him.

* Corrie ten Boom, *The Hiding Place*, Hodder and Stoughton, 2015, p195.

'If you come near me, Preacher,' he said in that tortured voice, 'I'll kill you.'

'You could do that,' I agreed. 'You could cut me in a thousand pieces and lay them out on the street and every piece would love you.'*

What was it that enabled David Wilkerson to love Nicky Cruz in this way? It was because he had experienced the same love from God. Jesus had already said to David Wilkerson, as he has said to each of us, 'You can reject me. You can betray me. You can ignore me. You can nail me to a cross. But still every part of me will say I love you.'

This kind of love is a love which changes the world. Martin Luther King said, 'only love can turn an enemy into a friend.' This is the reason why Paul ends this section talking about burning coals. It is a quotation from Proverbs which probably refers to the ancient Egyptian practice of carrying burning coals on one's head to signify remorse and the desire to live differently. Loving people radically changes people.

This is what happened with David Wilkerson and Nicky Cruz. This is what happened with Jackie Pullinger in the Walled City. This is the transformative effect of a love which is real in its authenticity, inclusivity and commitment. This is the love that changes the world.

This is not a love that we try to generate through our own hard work. We love one another not just in the same way that God loves us, but with the same love. The Holy Spirit is the one given to us in order that we might love other people in this way. He has been poured into our hearts so that this love might overflow into all our relationships, all our encounters, all our interactions. We are to simply pass on the radical, beautiful, inexplicable and unlimited love we have been given ourselves.

* David Wilkerson, *The Cross and the Switchblade*, Rickfords Hill Publishing, 2012, p77.

Chapter 18

ENGAGEMENT

*Let everyone be subject to the governing authorities, for there
is no authority except that which God has established. The
authorities that exist have been established by God.*

ROMANS 13:1

'He's the King. He's the Lord of the whole wood*.'

MR BEAVER

My father once did a talk at his church with the title, 'The Election:
How to Decide'. It went so badly that it was included in a book
called *Bad Sermons and Why they were Bad*,** which shows the risk
of trying to talk about the impact of faith on politics.

However, it is unavoidable because God's love changes everything.
It changes the way we relate to God, the way we relate to ourselves,
the way we relate to those around us, to family, friends, strangers
and enemies. It also changes the way we relate to society in general,
to the state, to those in government, and to politicians. The love of
God transforms the way we engage with politics and economics. It
affects how we vote.

God created the whole world, loves the whole world and is
involved in every part of the world. He is not just the God of the
spiritual parts of our lives: he is the God of all of life: its institutions,
its economy, and its politics. The Christian faith has serious
implications for the whole of society and its political and economic
structures. If we are to love other people we will have think about

* C.S. Lewis, *The Lion, the Witch and the Wardrobe*, HarperCollins, 2009, p87.
** Or so he claims. I have yet to find evidence that this book ever existed.

the environment in which they live, the structures that can either help or harm them, the opportunities they have or lack, the ways they are protected or left vulnerable.

So, if we love God and love one another, we should become more engaged in the things of the world, not less. For the love of God does not remove us from the world but connects us more deeply to it. It does not make us less interested in the world, but more interested. It should make us more likely to vote, more likely to enter politics, and more likely to be involved in the political process.

And so, Paul writes to the Christians in Rome about their relationship with the governing authorities. He wants those who lived in the most political city in the world, to know how their love for God and one another should shape their politics. For the love of God means engaging with our political process in a distinctive way.

RESPECT

First, the love of God means that we engage with respect. For every politician and government official is one who is loved by God.

Paul describes the governing authorities as 'servants of God' (13:4). He uses the same Greek word *diakonoi* that is used of deacons in the Church, those who serve as pastors, teachers, and evangelists. Paul appears to imply that the governing authorities are just as much servants of God for society as pastors, teachers and evangelists are within the Church.

This is a very good reason to enter politics if you are a Christian. It was passages in the Bible like these that persuaded the great reformer William Wilberforce to become an MP instead of becoming a clergyman in the Church of England. Many other Christians have been inspired by their faith to enter politics as a means of serving God and transforming society.

It also means respecting those politicians we disagree with, or who may be deeply flawed people. The Roman emperor at the time that Paul was writing was Nero. Nero poisoned his own mother, persecuted Christians and possibly started the Great Fire of Rome to clear space for his new palace. If the first Christians were supposed to respect Nero, then we must respect our politicians today.

It may be tempting to write off our politicians, despairing at their failings and flaws. But engaging in politics with respect means taking politicians seriously, listening properly to what they have to say and thinking deeply about the issues they are facing. It may mean confronting with respect, protesting with respect, campaigning against individuals, but with respect.

And it is worth remembering that it is more admirable to at least attempt to govern, than it is simply to criticize the people who do.

In his famous speech in Paris in 1910, the American President, Theodore Roosevelt, said,

> It is not the critic who counts; not the man who points out how the strong man stumbles, or where the doer of deeds could have done them better. The credit belongs to the man who is actually in the arena, whose face is marred by dust and sweat and blood; who strives valiantly; who errs, who comes short again and again, because there is no effort without error and shortcoming; but who does actually strive to do the deeds; who knows great enthusiasms, the great devotions; who spends himself in a worthy cause; who at the best knows in the end the triumph of high achievement, and who at the worst, if he fails, at least fails while daring greatly, so that his place shall never be with those cold and timid souls who neither know victory nor defeat.*

It is better to attempt to enter politics and fail, than to sit on the side criticizing. So, no matter how flawed our politicians might be, loving our world means that we engage with respect.

---

* Theodore Roosevelt, 'Citizenship in a Republic', address delivered at the Sorbonne, Paris, France, 23 April 1910.

REALISM

It also means that we engage with realism. For our politicians are *loved by* God; they are not themselves God.

In describing the governing authorities as 'servants of God' Paul is being deliberately subversive. Nero did not consider himself to be a 'servant of God'; he considered himself to *be* God. Paul was giving Nero a radical demotion, emphasizing that he is not as important as he thinks he is.

I find this helpful when it is a time to vote, because it means that I approach the question with realism. I recognize that all the candidates will be flawed, no one will represent me perfectly, and no one will be promoting all the policies that I would want them to promote. I don't need to find the perfect candidate or the perfect party. I might vote for someone who I disagree with on many issues but feel like they are the best option given the circumstances.

During elections, it seems common to hear each party or candidate claiming that if they win they will sort out all the problems in the country, but that if the other party were to win it would be a total disaster for the country. Other people say that it will make no difference who wins. But the truth is probably somewhere in the middle. It is normally neither irrelevant who wins an election, nor the only thing that matters. Realism means recognizing that politics has a role in shaping a nation, but it is not the only thing that shapes the nation. Politics is neither the only way to solve problems in society, but nor is it irrelevant. There are things that politicians can do, and there are things that charities and churches can do.

To change society, we need both politics and something more than politics. Changes take place through changes to laws, but we also need changed hearts. In 1964 the Civil Rights Act was passed in America and Martin Luther King won the Nobel Peace Prize. Immediately, he went to see the American President Lyndon Johnson and demanded a Voting Rights Act. However, Lyndon

Johnson was a pragmatic politician, telling Luther King that he had used all his political capital getting the Civil Rights Act through congress, and so the Voting Rights Act would be between five and ten years away.

Martin Luther King left that meeting, and instead of giving up and blaming politicians, went back to Selma, Alabama and started to organize a march from Selma to Montgomery. That march led to the confrontation on 'Bloody Sunday', in which the marchers were beaten and imprisoned. Two weeks later Christian leaders from all over the country swept to Selma, Alabama to stand with Martin Luther King for that march to Montgomery. As a result of that march, the Voting Rights Act was passed five months later. Change took place because of a combination of the actions of people and the work of politicians.

VISION

Third, the love of God means that we engage with vision. For God's love is a love that inspires. For, just as we are loved by God, so too is every person, every society, every nation. This gives us a vision for the world as it could be and should be.

In this part of his letter, Paul describes the governing authorities at their best rather than at their worst. He says that 'the one in authority is God's servant for your good' (13:4). This is the potential a politician has. Paul would have also been aware of their failings. He says that their role is to punish those who do wrong, when he knows that they have put Jesus, an innocent man, to death just a couple of decades earlier. But he describes their potential, seeing them with vision rather than cynicism.

It is easy to be cynical about politics and politicians, and so much political debate is characterized by negativity, where we try to spot mistakes, latching on to something we disagree with. But Paul's description of his own governing authorities inspires us to engage with hope and vision for what politics could be and should be.

For the Bible provides us not only with a vision for our personal life, but a vision for society. It contains encouragement, guidance, and strength for our private lives, but also for our nations. The Bible has a lot to say on the current political questions of injustice, immigration, race, debt, inequality, care for those in poverty, economics, warfare, business, and social cohesion. It gives us a vision for the kind of nation we want to build and the kind of communities we want to be part of.

FAITH

Finally, the love of God means we engage with faith, for love led Jesus to the cross and raised him from the dead.

Before he died, Jesus stood before a politician, Pontius Pilate. This weak and flawed politician made the worst and most unjust political decision ever made. He decided to put God himself to death, and in doing so chose what was popular over what was right, pleasing a pressure group instead of following his own conscience. Then Pilate called a vote that should never have been called, and the people voted unanimously for Barabbas over Jesus. It was the total failure of politics, and the greatest injustice in history. And yet, God worked through this political mistake to bring about the salvation of the world.

This is the source of our faith, and we can be confident that God is at work in all things, including our political processes. Ultimately, politicians do not decide the fate of our nations. Politicians come and go, kings and queens rise and fall, empires and nation states emerge and collapse, but Jesus remains Lord, and can bring about good in every situation.

So much of our political systems may be broken. Many of our politicians may be selfish, hard-hearted, and foolish. But how did Jesus respond to this weak politician who put him to death? Ultimately, he loved him, and he died for him. How did he respond to the crowd who called for his crucifixion? He loved them and died for them. The one who came to bring justice, and free people from oppression, also loved those who were guilty of injustice and oppression. This is the love that has the power to transform our politics, our politicians and the world.

Chapter 19

FIGHT

*And do this, understanding the present time: the hour has
already come for you to wake up from your slumber, because our
salvation is nearer now than when we first believed. The night
is nearly over; the day is almost here. So let us put aside the
deeds of darkness and put on the armour of light. Let us behave
decently, as in the daytime, not in carousing and drunkenness,
not in sexual immorality and debauchery, not in dissension and
jealousy. Rather, clothe yourselves with the Lord Jesus Christ, and
do not think about how to gratify the desires of the flesh.*

ROMANS 13:11-14

'You can't be dead. You can't be, because I love you. You hear
me, I love you. Now get up."

TRINITY TO NEO

When one of my sons was eight years old, I took him and four of his
friends to Lazerzone for his birthday. I found the whole experience
quite stressful. After we'd been given lazer guns and packs for our
chest and back, we were taken into a maze-like room, where there
was some intense music playing. I was told that my code name
was 'Zombie' which didn't help my mood, and I found myself
surrounded by five very small but accurate children running around
me shooting me and laughing.

I felt embarrassed. I felt like I didn't belong there. I wanted to
leave. But then something switched inside of me, and I realized I

---

* *The Matrix*, directed by The Wachowskis, Warner Bros., 1999.

needed to fight back. Suddenly, my son was no longer my son; his friends were no longer his friends; they were all quite simply 'the enemy'. From that moment I started to use all my superior height, weight, speed, and general life experience to try to hold my own. By the end of our session, I felt I had fought back fairly and not been outdone by the children.

We left the dark labyrinth, and began eating pizza and cake together in the lobby, as we waited for the scores to come in. Finally, the guy who worked there came out with the results, giving each person a score card based on the position they had come in. He started with sixth place, then moved up the ranks up to second place, giving the cards to the children I had been with. Then, with a look which combined contempt and disdain, he handed me my score card, confirming that I had managed to come first, beating the small children I was with, accumulating three times the number of points that any of them had.

The shame I felt got worse when I had to face the other parents on Monday morning at the school gates. I knew they were thinking sarcastically, 'Well done, Jonny. Thanks for thrashing my young, sensitive son at Lazerzone. I bet that makes you feel really good about yourself.' I wanted to hide, to disappear. And my only comfort was knowing that I was nowhere near as competitive as Tara would have been if she'd gone in my place.

Psychologists remind us that we are hardwired for struggle.* Something within us needs to fight. This can often be destructive, as we attack one another, verbally or physically. But it can also be constructive. For the Christian life is a battle. Living in the love of God means engaging in a series of battles. We are brought into an external battle against injustice, oppression, inequality, loneliness, and suffering. There is also a spiritual battle, against the spiritual forces of evil that operate in the world. But here, Paul turns his

* Brene Brown, 'The Power of Vulnerability', *TED Talks*, June 2010, www.ted.com.

attention to another kind of battle that each of us has to fight: the internal battle. This is the battle that God's love enables us to fight, and to win.

There is always a gap between the life we live and the life we would like to live, and between the decisions we make and the decisions we would like to make. After all, most people want to be good people, do the right thing, and make a positive difference to the people around them, but just find it difficult to live up to their own standards.

One obstacle is ignorance, not knowing what the right thing is. That is why we have the Bible which contains God's revelation of how to live (called 'the Law'). This is God's guidance on how to conduct our relationships, how to live selflessly, compassionately, wisely, and how to build a just society. But knowing what is good and right is not enough, for even if we know what we should do, it can be hard to find the motivation to do it. This is where love comes in.

For there are three main motivations for action. The first is *fear*. I have a friend who is diabetic, and he told me that when he injects himself with insulin some people say to him, 'I could never do that.' And he replies, 'Well, if you didn't you would die, so you would probably find that you could.' Fear of dying, failing, or missing out can be powerful motivation. The second is a *desire for a reward*. I often wonder what induces people to enter the world of heavyweight professional boxing and have someone hit them repeatedly while watched by millions of people. But then I remember that they can earn tens of millions of pounds in the process, and I wonder whether I should try it. Fear and desire for a reward are powerful forces (which is why politicians often appeal to these to win votes). However, there is a third driving force which is more powerful than either of them: *love*. For love is the greatest motivational force in the world. Love is what induces parents to go without sleep for their children, or children to run marathons for their parent's cancer treatment. Love is what enables an introvert husband to put on a party for his extrovert wife, or what motivates an extrovert writer to lock themselves away to study something that fascinates them. Love is what enables us to go beyond what we would naturally want to do.

When Paul says that 'love is the fulfilment of the Law' (13:10) he is not just saying that love sums up the Law, but that when we love God and love one another we are able to keep the Law. Elsewhere Paul writes, 'Christ's love compels us.'* Love is the driving force in our lives. Love is the power to do what is right. It's not that love makes us always *feel* like doing the right thing, but love makes it possible to do the right thing even when we don't feel like it, and to go beyond what we would normally be able to do.

Not long ago, Tara left our house early with our eldest child to go to school, leaving me to get the other three ready for school – getting them breakfast, making packed lunches, getting them dressed, teeth brushed, shoes on, so that when she got back everyone was ready to get to school. When she got back however, no one had brushed their teeth, only one had their shoes on, one of the packed lunches hadn't been made, and one of them was completely naked. Tara was understandably a bit annoyed that I hadn't managed to do everything, but I had the perfect defence. I told her, 'Tara, I did my best.' Which was true. I had done my best.

However, Tara replied, 'Okay. That's great you did your best, but our children cannot go to school without shoes on, or with nothing to eat for lunch, or completely naked. Jonny, with parenting, it's not enough to do your best; you have to do whatever it takes.'

It struck me that this is true of lots of the most important things in life. If you're about to have a lifesaving operation you don't really want the surgeon shrugging their shoulders and saying, 'I'll do my best' or a lawyer defending you when you've been wrongly accused

---

* 2 Corinthians 5:14.

of a serious crime saying, 'These things are always difficult, but I'll do my best.' You want them to say, 'I'll do whatever it takes.'

And when you love someone, you do whatever it takes. When God saw the sin of the world, in his love he decided to do whatever it takes, even though that meant coming to this earth and dying on a cross.

God's love is like a new energy source in our lives. Becoming a Christian means switching the power source of your life. We may have the same job, the same relationships, even the same ambitions, but the driving force in our lives is transformed because we have the love of God within us.

Paul then uses two images to describe how this works: waking up and getting dressed. We need to wake up to fight. And we need to get dressed to fight.

WAKE UP

First, we need to wake up to fight.

In the early stages of dating, Tara and I went to stay with some friends. I got up earlier than her and decided I would bring her a cup of tea in bed. I entered her bedroom as quietly as I could, approached her gently, whispering softly to her, 'Tara, Tara.' She opened her eyes with a look of terror at my face so close to hers, and instinctively jabbed me in the neck with her hand. Her first instinct on waking up was to try to kill me.

Paul says, 'The hour has already come for you to wake up from your slumber' (13:11). It is almost as if our problem is not so much that we are insufficiently good, but that we are insufficiently awake. So much of the mess we get into, whether personally or culturally, comes not only from conscious decisions to do the wrong thing, but from attitudes and practices of which some are unconscious. We can be unaware of the injustice and oppression that exists around us, and our own parts in the structures and practices that cause them. Or we can find ourselves unconsciously putting work ahead of family, or drifting into a relationship that's bad for us, or wasting our life on something that is unfulfilling. We can easily find ourselves sleepwalking to disaster.

But God's love has the power to wake us up, to shake us, to jolt us out of the things we've got ourselves into. It may be through friends pointing things out to us that we hadn't been aware of, a verse from the Bible that challenges us, a moment that shows us the foolishness of our course of action.

God's love is not just a love that comforts and encourages and secures; it's also a love that challenges and confronts and wakes us up. Jesus is the light of the world, and light is an image of guidance, wisdom and knowledge, but also of waking from sleep as the sun comes up. Jesus came into the world to wake us from our slumber.

At the end of the film *The Matrix*, when Neo has been killed by Agent Smith, Trinity says to him, 'You can't be dead. You can't be, because I love you. You hear me, I love you. Now get up.'* And he gets up and fights again.

God says something similar to you and me. He says, 'I love you. You hear me, I love you. Now get up.' And then we get up and fight.

GET DRESSED

Paul moves from the image of waking up to the image of getting dressed. He writes about putting off deeds of darkness and putting on the armour of light, and of clothing ourselves with Christ (13:12).

In writing about clothing, Paul is pointing back to the beginning of the Bible where Adam and Eve rebelled against God, when sin entered the world, and as a result they felt shame. They felt incomplete, insecure, inadequate, covering themselves with fig leaves due to the discomfort they felt with themselves. They were attempting to cover the internal shame with external garments.

* *The Matrix*, 1999.

This is a universal problem. We are always trying to cover ourselves, to compensate for the shame we feel inside. Paul lists six deeds of darkness (which he links in three sets of pairs, 13:13), representing the ways we compensate for our internal inadequacies. The language he uses may seem extreme, but they represent things that almost all of us struggle with in some way.

We cover our shame by trying to *consume* ('carousing and drunkenness'). We look to substances to make us feel better. We hope that food, alcohol, drugs or pleasure will fill what we sense is lacking within. Or we try to *cling* ('sexual immorality and debauchery'). We look to other people to satisfy what is lacking within us, using people and relationships to fulfil us. Finally, we *compete* ('jealousy and dissension'). We blame, criticize, compare or try to beat everyone else to make ourselves feel better.

However, if we are clothed with Christ (13:14) we do not need to turn to any of these things to be complete. He covers our shame. He makes us whole. He alone is the one who gives you worth.

And we are given more than just clothing. Paul says to put on 'armour' (13:12). Actually, the Greek word *hopla* refers more accurately to 'weapons'. We are supposed to be putting on the weapons of light.

I had a friend who worked in advertising, doing some work with a major manufacturer of chewing gum. They told him that they needed his help to work out how to persuade people to eat more chewing gum. He replied that this was the wrong approach. It would be better for them to work out how to get people to *carry* more gum, because when you carry gum, you eat it; when you don't, you don't.

I think this is true of many areas of our lives. We use what we carry. When I have my phone with me, I check it too often. When I have water with me, I drink enough water. When I have chocolate with me, I eat too much chocolate. We use what we have with us. This is the reason why, in the UK, it is a criminal offense to carry weapons, even if you have no intention of using them, because if something were to happen you would very likely use what you were carrying.

On my twenty-first birthday, a friend of mine gave me a full-length replica of Gandalf's sword from *The Lord of the Rings*. I have sometimes carried it from our house to church to use it as a sermon illustration, feeling quite conspicuous holding this huge sword as I walk and aware that it is an offensive weapon. And each time I have walked through the streets with it, I have thought to myself, 'Please may this be the day that somebody tries to mug me?' Just so that I can get it out and say, 'Are you serious?'

What are you carrying? When faced with the battles of life, what are you carrying with you?

Every morning, before I do anything else I try to spend some time reading the Bible and praying, because I want to start the day with Jesus, so that he is the one I am carrying into my day. I don't know what I will come across, whether it will be temptation, disappointment, or tragedy, so I want to make sure that I am carrying the right equipment from the start. I know that if I start my day with social media, I will likely carry into the day comparison, jealousy and insecurity. If I start my day with the news, I'll most likely carry into the day conflict, despair and cynicism. If I start the day just with myself, I will carry confusion, fear and inadequacy. But if I start with God and his love for me, I will carry his promises, his strength, his wisdom, his encouragement, his comfort, his grace, and I will be able to face whatever comes at me. I don't want to go naked into the battlefield of life. I want to go in armed to the teeth with all that God has for me so that I can face whatever may come.

I have done this almost every morning since I was a teenager, before I get dressed, before I have breakfast, before I face the world. This is how I wake up from my spiritual slumber, move from fantasy to reality, weakness to power, confusion to clarity, emptiness to fulfilment, fear to faith, insecurity to confidence. Starting to read the Bible for myself each morning in my early teens marked the start of the development of my own faith, where I opened up myself to God's loving voice for me, and the power of God's love to live the life that he wanted me to live. God's love clothes us and equips us. It wakes us up. It enables us to fight for what it right.

Chapter 20

UNITY

Accept one another, then, just as Christ accepted you, in order to bring praise to God.

ROMANS 15:7

'Love is the drive towards the unity of the separate.'*

PAUL TILLICH

We live in a divided world, with divisions between nations and within nations, between communities and within communities, in families, political parties, churches, and businesses. Division tears apart marriages, breaks up families, and destroys communities. At its worst, division manifests itself as segregation, apartheid, or civil war.

Paul was writing to a church struggling with division. Rome was a global city, containing people of rich and poor, young and old, with different nationalities, political views, and philosophical positions. In particular, the Church in Rome had to deal with the tension between Jewish and Gentile Christians. This conflict is possibly the main reason that Paul wrote the letter.

In much of what he has been saying up to this point Paul has been laying the groundwork for dealing with the divisions there, and now he addresses the issue head on. The controversy centred on which foods they should be allowed to eat, and which days of the week you could do various things. These may not be the main issues you're facing today, but the way that Paul deals with these

---

* Paul Tillich, *Love, Power, and Justice: Ontological Analyses and Ethical Applications*, Oxford University Press, 1954, p25.

issues teaches us about how to overcome divisions that we face for ourselves.

A major source of division comes from our inability to deal with difference. Whenever you have two people or two groups of people (whether they are two friends, a husband and wife, a boss and employee, a liberal and conservative) you are confronted by their differences, whether in personality, beliefs, or politics. When we are confronted with these differences it seems like there are four main approaches we can take.

MODEL 1: AVOIDING

The first approach is for you to try to stay in your box, and they in theirs.

Philosophically you might say, 'You have your truth and I have my truth.' Practically, you might say, 'You do your thing and I'll do my thing.' A family might find themselves all watching different content on separate screens because they can't agree on what they would watch together. Housemates might decide on having separate shelves in the fridge and separate shelves in the cupboard, so that they can each shop and cook in their own way and at a time that suits them. And when we fall out with someone, we end up simply avoiding them and attempting to live separate lives. This model means saying, 'My life is my business and has no impact on your life, so let me do my own thing and I'll let you do your thing.'

This approach can sometimes be helpful in the short term (if we need to cool off after an argument). However, in the long term it leads to increasing isolation and loneliness in our society, for individualism ultimately leads to indifference.

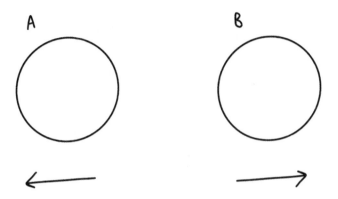

Consequently, we grow further apart, increasingly struggling to show empathy towards anyone different to ourselves, and our culture becomes characterized by people shouting at each other from greater and greater distances.

Paul challenges this approach by insisting that we are not disconnected, for we are one body, connected to one another as a body is connected to itself (12:5). We are brothers and sisters (14:10), we should consider the impact of our actions for one another (14:15) and longing for a unity where they might glorify God with 'one mind and one voice' (15:6). What we do is not just our own business because we are one body. Every action has an impact on others in the body. If it doesn't have an immediate effect on someone else, it affects us, and we have an effect on other people. So, Paul tells the Church in Rome not just to think about their own actions, their own consciences, but how their actions have an impact on other people.

Avoidance is not the way that God deals with division. The problem with the world is that it is attempting to disconnect and divide itself from its creator, but God's response is not to say, 'You do your thing and I'll do my thing, and let's keep out of each other's way.' For God loves us and love desires closeness, connection, unity. God's love brought him close and continues to long for connection with those he loves.

MODEL 2: SHRINKING

I once had some training on dealing with conflict in which we were told that conflict emerges from the fact that we all have core beliefs, which we hold on to strongly, and peripheral beliefs, about which we are more flexible. We were told that conflict takes place when our core beliefs clash with other people's core beliefs, so the best way to deal with conflict is to move things from our core beliefs into our peripheral beliefs, so that we believe fewer and fewer things, less and less strongly.

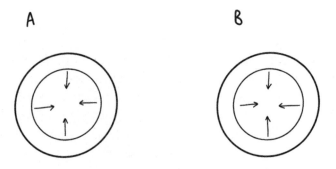

Again, there is a degree of truth in this approach, in that it is important to establish what matters and what doesn't, what is certain and what is not. Paul reminds the Church in Rome not to get distracted by what he calls 'disputable matters' (14:1). I do not believe that Jesus had a small set of core beliefs, nor that his strong set of core beliefs made him bad at conflict.

The key to unity is not ensuring that we all believe fewer and fewer things, less and less strongly. The consequence of this approach would be that we become a reduced version of ourselves in the attempt to accommodate other people. This approach says, 'I've learnt not to care' or 'Whatever you want, Darling' or 'It won't make any difference anyway', or 'I've found it best not to have an opinion on this'.

If we follow this path, we end up losing our convictions, our passions, and our beliefs, to keep the peace. We become less. However, Paul says to the Roman Church that they are to 'be fully convinced in their own mind' (14:5). Disunity is not created by people having passionate views. It is created by failing to love one another despite our different, passionately held views.

God does not ask us to become less passionate to bring unity. God overcame the distance between himself and humanity, not by becoming less, but by coming to us completely in Jesus Christ. The Word became flesh and dwelt among us, but he did not cease to be God in the process. He bridged the gap while remaining himself. He prayed 'not my will, but yours be done',* but he did not cease to have a will. He gave up his life on the cross, but he did not give up his identity.

MODEL 3: ATTACKING

The third approach is the one that seems increasingly to be the dominant means of dealing with difference in our society. On this model the way to deal with difference or disagreement by attempting to eradicate it. Individuals and groups try to attack and destroy any opposition, as seen in the growing hostility, abuse and polarization of debate in our society, particularly political debate. And so, people end up being afraid to say what they think for fear of abuse.

The journalist and writer Caitlin Moran commented on this,

Language has been so corrupted and turbo-charged with emotion that I do not think we can call it language any more. Language is for conveying information, starting debates, trying to make things, build solutions. That is not what is going on here. What these people are speaking in is, instead, 'langrage'.

Langrage is not for discussions, or whimsy, or musing, or asking questions: it is fashioned and purposed for blitz. Its intent is to belittle or destroy. It treats communication as something primarily devoted to warfare and believes anything is allowable so long as it means you 'win'.

This is dialogue turned into a shoot-em-up game – 'langrage' is the weaponisation of words. Born on the internet, and now ported into politics, it's more systemic than 'trolling'. It's the language of rage. And it is, increasingly, the language of our age.**

* Luke 22:42.
** Caitlin Moran, 'Hate Speak is All the Rage', *The Times Magazine*, 17 December 2016, speech.almeida.co.uk.

I heard this account from another journalist who was visiting Goa in India and started a conversation with another global visitor in a yoga class, who was wearing a tee-Shirt with the 'Om' sign on it (signifying unity, oneness and peace). After an hour of yoga chanting 'om', they got talking about the violence in her own country and terrible consequences of the conflicts there. She said to the reporter, 'You know all the divisions and conflict in my country could be finished in a day if only we did one thing.' 'What's that?' the reporter asked her, intrigued. 'All we have to do' she said, 'is kill our enemies more ruthlessly and then they will give up.' Slightly taken aback the reporter asked her, 'How does that fit with the tee-shirt you're wearing with its symbol of peace and oneness?' 'Oh that?' she replied, 'That's just for yoga.'

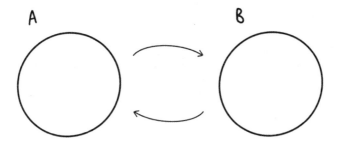

Either we try to destroy our opponents, or we try to prevent them from expressing their views. The desired consequence of this approach is the removal of the other person and the destruction of difference. As someone once said of their marriage, 'My husband and I are one. And I am that one.'

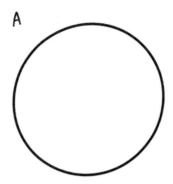

A

Again, Paul challenges this approach, arguing that we are not to simply please ourselves and so risk destroying one another but 'should please our neighbours for their good, *to build them up*' (15:2). For it is not enough to be right, we also need to be loving. Whether in an argument with a friend, a disagreement at work, or a political debate, there is being right, and there is communicating our position in a way that is loving. Paul forbids us from judging one another (14:3), instead insisting on treating one another with respect. He reminds them that they are brothers and sisters (14:9), neighbours (15:2), people who are valuable and loved by God.

MODEL 4: EMBRACING

Paul says that there is another approach to unity, which involves neither avoiding, shrinking, or attacking the other. He writes, 'accept one another as Christ has accepted you' (15:7).

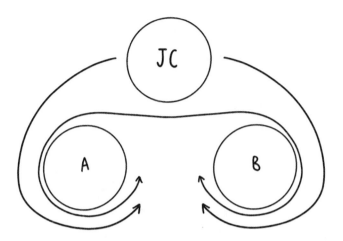

Paul introduces another person into the conflict. It is not just about person A and person B, or group A and group B, for Jesus is now brought into the situation. There is another actor in the drama, who changes the whole dynamic. For Paul says that Jesus has 'accepted you'. 'Accepted' means more than tolerated; it means 'welcomed', 'brought close'. Jesus brings us close. He welcomes the lepers, the beggars, the unpopular rich and the despised poor. He says, 'let the little children come to me."* And Paul is saying that we need to accept one another in the same way. The welcome we have received from God is supposed to be the inspiration and energy with which we welcome one another.

The key to unity is not keeping people at a distance, nor becoming less yourself, nor attempting to destroy the opposition, but respecting, honouring, and welcoming people, bringing them close. For it's hard to hate people when you see them up close.

* Mark 10:14.

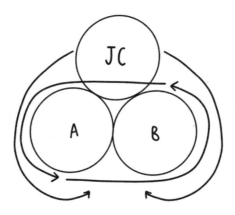

There is often a cost to this. You cannot welcome someone into your life without changing in some way. When Tara and I were dating it was clear that her life was very ordered and mine was quite chaotic, and so in getting married we had to accept that it would mean Tara embracing more chaos than she thought was healthy, and me accepting more order than I thought was necessary. Similarly, you cannot welcome children into your life and expect your life to stay the same. It requires sacrifice to bring them close. This is how God has loved us and destroyed the divisions between us: by laying down his life for us in order that we might be perfectly united to him.

The Bible emphasizes both the distance and the closeness between God and humanity. God is perfect; we are imperfect. God is Spirit; we are physical. God is Holy; we are sinful. But in Jesus Christ this difference has been overcome. The greatest distance has been replaced by the greatest possible unity.

Paul is saying that if God has overcome the greatest distance that could ever exist, it must be possible for us to be united among ourselves. If God can overcome the difference between perfect divinity and sinful humanity, can he not also overcome the difference between introverts and extroverts, or liberals and conservatives, young and old? We might say, 'But we're too different', but there is no greater difference than between us and God and he has overcome that difference. We might say, 'But we've drifted too far apart,' but there is no greater distance than between heaven and earth and God has overcome that distance and brought unity. We might say, 'Too much has happened which cannot be undone,' but God has forgiven the unforgivable in us which enables us to forgive the unforgivable in one another. God has bridged the unbridgeable gap and made all gaps bridgeable.

This is the only hope for unity in the Church. This is the only basis of our unity in the Church. Don Carson put it like this:

> The reason there are so many exhortations in the New Testament for Christians to love other Christians is because ... the church itself is not made up of natural 'friends'. It is made up of natural enemies. What binds us together is not common education, common race, common income levels, common politics, common nationality, common accents, common jobs, or anything else of that sort. Christians come together not because they form a natural collocation, but because they have all been saved by Jesus Christ and owe him a common allegiance. In this light we are a band of natural enemies who love one another for Jesus' sake.[*]

WORKING HARD AT UNITY

Unity is still hard work. Paul says, 'Make every *effort* to do what leads to peace and to mutual edification' (14:19). Unity is not always obvious and won't always feel natural. Sometimes we cannot see how we can find a place for people who seem so different.

---

[*] Don Carson, quoted in Timothy Keller, 'The Fading of Forgiveness', *Comment*, 16 September 2021, cardus.ca.

When we first moved into our house in Brighton, we didn't have a fridge, so we ordered a new one. When it arrived, we discovered that it was too big to go along the corridor, down our stairs and into the kitchen in the basement. The delivery man left it by the door, telling us that we could try to take the doors off and then reattach them if we wanted, or we could send it back, and then he left, leaving us with a fridge that didn't fit in our house on our doorstep.

We tried to work out what to do: send it back or attempt to dismantle it and put it back together. Then some friends came round and one of them suggested a third option, which was to take the fridge back out of the door, down the steps on to the street, along the pavement to the end of the road, round the corner, lift it over a small wall into our neighbour's front garden, lift it over some iron railings, on to a ledge and then lower it into our sunken front garden into the flower bed below, then take it through the garden, entering our house by the back door. It seemed a little complicated, but we said, 'Okay. Let's give it a go', aware that any damage would mean we weren't able to return it. So, we took it out of the house, down some steps, round the front of the house, along the road, round the corner, over a wall into our neighbour's front garden, then over some iron railings, on to a ledge, then lowered it down into the flower bed in our sunken garden, walked it through the garden and in through the garden doors into the kitchen. Remarkably, it worked, and when we got it into the kitchen, we discovered that there was a perfect space for it.

When people come into your life it can sometimes feel like there's no space for them. They are too different, and you can't see how they could possibly fit. But it just takes a bit of imagination, and a bit of effort and a few people to help you, and suddenly you find a way to bring them close and discover that there was a perfect place for them in your life all along.

This is what God has done for us and this is the hope for unity in a divided and isolated world: the love of God which has brought us close and enables us to bring others close to us.

Chapter 21

PURPOSE

… the grace God gave me to be a minister of Christ Jesus to the Gentiles. He gave me the priestly duty of proclaiming the gospel of God, so that the Gentiles might become an offering acceptable to God, sanctified by the Holy Spirit.

ROMANS 15:15-16

'All we have to decide is what to do with the time that is given us.'*

GANDALF

According to the Harvard Negotiation Project, people tend to have five core concerns: *autonomy* (the desire to make one's own choices and be in control of one's fate), *appreciation* (the desire to be recognized and valued), *affiliation* (the desire to be accepted and belong to a group), *status* (the desire to know where you stand) and *role* (the desire to have a meaningful purpose).**

We have seen how the love of God answers each of the first four desires. It gives us autonomy, for God's love sets us free to be ourselves. It gives us appreciation, for it affirms our value. It gives us affiliation, for it connects us to God and to one another. And it gives us status, because it establishes us as children of God.

And now we are going to see how it fulfils our desire for a role, for the love of God gives us meaningful purpose. For Paul writes of '*the grace that God gave me* to be a minister of Christ Jesus to

---

* J.R.R. Tolkien, *The Fellowship of the Ring*, HarperCollins, 1994, p50.
** Roger Fisher and William Ury, *Getting to Yes*, Random House, 2012, p32.

the Gentiles' (15:15–16). His purpose (being a minister of Jesus to the Gentiles) came from 'grace'. God's grace, his unconditional, undeserved kindness and goodness, saves us and then it sends us.

This was Paul's experience. Jesus met him on the road to Damascus, and not only revealed himself to him, but also called him. Paul was saved and sent all at once. The love of God welcomes us in and then sends us out. For his love for us is too much to be contained within us. It overflows. It needs to be shared. It is so powerful that it propels us out to the world around us.

At the very start of his letter Paul addresses the Church in Rome as 'those who are *loved* by God and *called* to be saints' (1:7). We are loved and we are called. Love and purpose belong together. And the order is significant, for it is not purpose that leads to love, but love that leads to purpose. You are not loved because of your purpose; your purpose is the consequence of being loved. If you look for a great purpose, hoping that it will make you loved, you will always be trying to prove yourself, but if your purpose emerges from being loved, it will flow from a deep security with you.

God's love is the spark that initiates your purpose. It is the energy that sustains you in your purpose. Ultimately, it is goal of your purpose, for it will remain for eternity. And as the love of God is the basis of your purpose, it means that your purpose is individual, surprising, and difficult.

INDIVIDUAL

God's love for us is specific and individual. And therefore, his purpose for our lives is specific and individual.

Being brought into a relationship with the God who loves us means entering a life of purpose. There are some things which are universal to all Christians, and other things that God has uniquely called each of us to do. When Paul refers to 'the priestly duty' (15:16), he is describing something that applies to all who follow Jesus. In the Old Testament priests helped the people of Israel to reconnect to God. In the New Testament all the people of God are described as priests.* So now, we are all called to help the world to reconnect with our creator. Just as priests in the Old Testament enabled the Israelites to make sacrifices (representing gratitude for everything they had been given, the receiving of forgiveness and the giving of the worshipper to God), so now our purpose is to help everyone to recognize what they've received from God, accept his forgiveness, and give themselves completely to God.

At a wedding the bridesmaids and ushers have the important role of helping the bride and groom to give themselves completely to the other, so that each of them can stand before someone who loves them completely and say to the other, 'All I am I give to you and all I have I share with you.'** In the same way, our purpose is to help one another to stand before the God who loves us and has given all things to us, and say to him, 'All I am I give to you and all I have I share with you.'

This is our general calling. But Paul is also aware of a specific calling that God has given to him to be 'a minister to the Gentiles' (15:16). He has a strong sense that there is a particular group that he is meant to go to, and that he needs to fulfil a particular role, which involves planting churches.

God has a specific purpose for your life. Just as God does not just love humanity in general but also you in particular, in the same way God, not only has a general purpose for humanity, but also a particular purpose for your life. No one else has your experience, your passions, your character, or your opportunities. God has things for you to do that only you can do.

Therefore, everyone is needed. Everyone counts. One of my favourite parts of the Bible are the lists of names. There are quite a lot of them in the Old Testament, and you find a few at the end of Paul's letters. They might not seem like the most interesting parts of

* 1 Peter 2:4–5.
** Marriage Service, Common Worship.

the Bible, but I love them because they remind me that God loves us individually and has a purpose for us individually.

The list at the end of Romans is interesting for several reasons. We read about Ampliatus, Urbanus, Hermes, Philologus and Julia, which were common names for slaves. But then there is also Narcissus, who was friends with the Emperor Claudius, and Aristobulus, who was grandson of Herod the Great and also friend of the Emperor. There are men and women, Jews and Gentiles, those in slavery and those who are free. Each of them matters and each of them has a purpose.

History has often been recorded as the story of either great individuals or of nameless masses. We learn that Napoleon invaded Russia in 1812, or that 'the peasants' revolted in England in 1381. When we think about the people around us it is difficult to think of everyone as individuals with their own stories. Our minds do not have the capacity to treat everyone as individuals, so we often think in terms of categories ('the elderly', 'the homeless', 'the French', 'politicians'), grouping people according to age, job, race, politics, or ability. However, God does not fulfil his purposes just through great individuals, nor through categories. He alone has the capacity to see us all individually. And this is reflected in the lists of names in the Bible. They remind us that everybody counts. Everyone is loved. Everyone has a purpose for their lives.

You have a specific calling on your life that God wants and needs you to do. It might not seem great, and maybe no one will notice, but ultimately this is how the world is changed. Governments are important, businesses and charities play important roles, and some people may even make a name for themselves, but by far the most powerful force in the world are the individual acts of people, unseen to all but God.

As George Eliot put in the final line of her novel, *Middlemarch*, describing her heroine, Dorothea,

> But the effect of her being on those around her was incalculably diffusive: for the growing good of the world is partly dependent on unhistoric acts; and that things are not so ill with you and me as they might have been is half owing to the number who lived faithfully a hidden life, and rest in unvisited tombs.*

SURPRISING

God's love for us means that his purpose for us is often surprising. For our purpose is not based on what everyone else is doing, what people think we should do, or even what we think we should do. It is based on a force that is external, but then begins to well up within us, and propels us in surprising directions.

Paul was called to be a minister to the Gentiles, and he must have felt like he was an unusual choice of a missionary to non-Jews. Paul was the most Jewish of Jews, with impeccable Jewish credentials, obeying the Jewish law obsessively, a Pharisee, and yet God called him to go to the non-Jews.

God's choice of people in the Bible is nearly always surprising. Moses struggled to speak in public and was a fugitive from Egypt for murder, so God called him to go back to Egypt to be Israel's spokesman. Gideon was weak and afraid, and God called him to lead a rebellion against the Midianites. Jonah detested Assyrians, and so God called him to preach in their capital. God's call on our life is rarely what we expect. Moses was not the most obvious person to go to Egypt. Gideon was not the most obvious person to lead a rebellion. The Virgin Mary not the most obvious person to have a baby.

---

* George Eliot, *Middlemarch*, Penguin Classics, 2011, p838.

We see the same thing throughout the history of the Church. D.L. Moody was an uneducated American evangelist who left school aged thirteen, and yet he led the mission to Cambridge University in 1882 that changed the course of the nation. David Wilkerson was a country pastor who knew nothing of city life, but he was called to the gangs of New York in the 1950s. Jackie Pullinger was a music student in London when God called her to the triad gangs and heroin addicts of Hong Kong in the 1960s. None of them were the obvious choice and yet God chose them.

I'm still so surprised that I spent thirteen years in Brighton. Brighton is edgy, sociable, and people seem to have lots of tattoos. Whereas I am conventional, introverted and like listening to BBC Radio 4. Now we find ourselves moving as a family to Rio de Janeiro and I don't feel like I'm the obvious candidate to be a missionary to the birthplace of Samba.

Of course, God uses our natural abilities, experience and passions. But he also works in our weaknesses and in unexpected ways. So, if you want to discover God's purpose for your life, instead of trying to find the perfect fit for your personality and passions, listen to the voice of God who loves you more than you can imagine, and which leads you in surprising directions. And you can trust these surprising directions because you know that God loves you and will never stop loving you wherever he sends you.

DIFFICULT

Any relationship, project or vision for anything that is born of love is difficult. Loving anyone is always harder but better than we imagine. This is true of marriage, of parenting, of deep friendship and true community. It's also true of planting churches, or starting businesses, and of anything else worthwhile. It is almost always harder, but almost always greater than we imagine. God's purpose for our lives, born out of his love for us, is always harder but greater than we imagine.

Paul knows that his purpose is to be 'a minister', a servant. The purpose God gives him is one that is for the sake of other people. Paul will give up his reputation, his relationships, and ultimately his life for the purpose that God gave him. When Paul first encounters Jesus, God speaks to a Christian called Ananias, and tells him to visit Paul because 'this man is my chosen instrument to carry my name before the Gentiles and their kings and before the people of Israel.' Then he adds, 'I will show him how much he must suffer for my name.'*

We discover our purpose, not by searching for something which will serve our own happiness and fulfilment, but by serving the God who loves us and desires our happiness and fulfilment. And this often has a cost for us. For this is how God has loved us, laying down his life for us. He loves us sacrificially, and this sacrificial love enables us to love one another sacrificially.

Paul's letter to the Romans has had an extraordinary impact on men and women in the history of the church. It led to the conversion of St Augustine, the greatest theologian in the history of the church. It sparked the Reformation through its impact on Martin Luther. It was transformational for John Wesley, leading to what became known as the Great Awakening. It sparked a theological revolution in the twentieth century through its influence on Karl Barth. But Paul could never have imagined any of this. In his mind he was just writing a letter to the Christian community in Rome because they were arguing about which foods they were allowed to eat.

* Acts 9:15–16.

TO BE AND TO LOVE

Paul starts his letter by reminding the Roman Christians that they were those who 'are loved by God and called *to be* saints' (1:7). More important than what we are called to do is who we are called to be. Often, I find myself asking God what I should be doing, when he seems to be interested in who I am becoming. For the call 'to be' is more important than the call to do. But even greater than the calling to be, is the calling to love.

I have four children and every day there are all kinds of things that I want to get them to do: get dressed, brush their teeth, go to school and be helpful. But much more important to me than any of these things is their character, who they are becoming. And the reason for most of what we try to get them to do is to help form their characters, so that they are responsible, kind, helpful, considerate people with clean teeth. But even more important than who they are becoming is their relationships – our relationship with them as parents to children, their relationships with each other and with friends, and more than anything else their relationship with the God who loves them. In the same way, God has a unique, surprising, difficult but significant purpose for each of us to do, but more important than what we do is who we are becoming, and even more important than who we are becoming is our love for him and one another. That is our ultimate and greatest and eternal purpose.

DISRUPTION

God's love for us turns our life around. Before he met Jesus, Paul had a purpose for his life: to imprison and kill Christians to protect the integrity of Judaism as he understood it. Paul was literally going in the wrong direction, attempting to do the wrong thing. But then Jesus came in his life, suddenly and dramatically, and turned his life around. From that moment on his purpose would be to serve Jesus the Messiah, who loved him and gave himself for him, to be holy, and to love God and those around him.

We never had any plans to leave Brighton. I love Brighton. I love England. I love its climate, the stony beaches, the English language, the English sense of humour, cricket, rugby, the English countryside. However, suddenly a new idea emerged for us: Brazil. This was not at all what I expected or thought I would want. All our married life had been spent in Brighton. We were settled there. And yet we have become convinced that God is now calling us to go to Rio de Janeiro for the next years of our lives. This call has disrupted our lives, and sent us in a new direction, for a new adventure. The only reason we feel confident to do this, is that we know that God loves us, that he is with us, and that he knows what he is doing.

When Jesus comes into our lives it may not be as sudden or dramatic as it was for Paul, but it is always disruptive. For his love for us secures and comforts us, but it also sends and redirects us. It is not always easy. But it is the greatest adventure there is.

PART SIX

Responding to God's Love (3)
ROMANS 16

Chapter 22

DELIGHTING IN THE LOVE OF GOD

Now to him who is able to establish you in accordance with my gospel, the message I proclaim about Jesus Christ, in keeping with the revelation of the mystery hidden for long ages past, but now revealed and made known through the prophetic writings by the command of the eternal God, so that all the Gentiles might come to the obedience that comes from faith – to the only wise God be glory forever through Jesus Christ! Amen.

ROMANS 16:25−27

'Beauty will save the world."

FYODOR DOSTOEVSKY

In 1975, Taibi Kahler identified five common drivers that motivate us: Be Perfect, Be Strong, Hurry Up, Please Others and Try Hard. These drivers are born in our unconsciousness and result in both beneficial and destructive behaviours. I think I'm motivated most by Please Others and Be Perfect, which means I try to do everything right in a way that keeps everyone happy. These may be our natural motivations, but Paul ends his letter by returning to his ultimate motivation for everything he does, which is the glory of God.

Paul spends much of the final part of his letter sending messages to and from his friends and co-workers, but he ends the letter by

* Fyodor Dostoevsky, *The Idiot*, translated by Constance Garnett,
Bantam Books, 1981, p370.

turning his attention again to God. He has lots of plans, things he wants to achieve, but more than anything else he longs for the glory of God. God's glory is the motivation for Paul's preaching of the Gospel so 'that all the Gentiles might come to the obedience that comes from faith' (16:26).

In the Greek these three verses are just one sentence, and commentators have suggested that the Greek here isn't very good grammatically. Far be it for me to criticize St Paul's Greek, which was much better than mine is, but it seems like he may have got overexcited at this point and ends up trying to fit more into one sentence than is natural or sensible, as he returns to lots of the themes of his letter – the Gospel, faith leading to obedience, revelation and mystery, God's power and wisdom. But it is understandable, for the reason he gets over-excited is that he is now thinking about the glory of God.

The glory of God is God's infinite beauty, his visible goodness. It is what makes him inherently loveable. We love God because of what he has done for us: his grace, forgiveness, kindness, provision, guidance, transformation, and inspiration. We love God as a response to his love for us. However, we also love God because he is inherently loveable. There is something in the very nature of God which is beautiful and deserves to be loved.

And yet we have turned our attention away from what is truly beautiful. At the beginning of his letter Paul insisted that we had exchanged the glory of God for images (1:23). He was writing to a community in a city where seeking one's own glory was everything. Today, we are also often obsessed with our own glory, wanting to be noticed, followed, liked, honoured, adored. But Jesus has come to redirect our hearts to God's glory, for that is an essential way that we love God in response to his love for us.

NEED-LOVE, GIFT-LOVE AND APPRECIATIVE LOVE

In *The Four Loves*, C.S. Lewis initially divides love into three dimensions: the need-love, the gift-love and the appreciative love. The *need-love* is the longing we have for someone or something when we love them or it. I love time by myself. I miss it if I don't have it. It is the need-love. The *gift-love* is the desire to care for the one we love. It is seen in the love of a parent for a child, wanting to do everything to provide for them and ensure they are happy. And the *appreciative love* is where we consider someone or something to be amazing, valuable, beautiful in and of itself. I love Roger Federer, one of the greatest tennis players of all time, in this way. My love for him is not the need-love, for it's not as if I don't think I will be able to live without him. It is not the gift-love, for I imagine he is quite comfortable without my support. It is the appreciative love because I think he plays tennis beautifully and I count it an honour to have lived at a time when I have been able to watch him play.

Now, to love someone completely means loving them in all three ways. I love Tara with a need-love in that I don't know how I would live without her. I would often be quite literally lost without her in my life. I love her with the gift-love in the sense that I want to provide for her, support and encourage her and do everything I can to make her happy. And I love her with the appreciative love in that I think she is an extraordinary person, and it is an honour to have met her, let alone to have got to marry her.

God loves us in each of these three ways. He loves us with a need-love. Even though he lacks nothing, he has created us in such a way that he finds his heart yearning for us. He misses us when we are far from him. We can break his heart by rejecting him and trying to live life without him. He is like the father in the story of the prodigal son, waiting and longing for his children to come home.* He loves us with a gift love, for 'God so loved the world that he *gave*

---

* Luke 15:20.

his one and only Son that whoever believes in him shall not perish but have eternal life.* He loves us graciously and self-sacrificially, giving us all things out of his love for us. And God loves us with an appreciative love, for he delights in us.** He considers us to be beautiful. He appreciates us for who we are.

This is how God loves us and this is how we are supposed to love God. We love him with a need-love, for we are lost without him. This is faith, where we receive the love and grace that we would be lost and dead without. We love him with a gift-love, offering our bodies as a living sacrifice. This is worship, where we give ourselves to the one who gave himself to us. And we love him with an appreciative love for he is worthy of love for his own sake.

LOVE AND GLORY

The reason, ultimately, why we love God in all these ways is his glory. This is why we need him, why we give to him, and why we appreciate him.

Need-Love

God's glory is the reason we need him. In Exodus 33 we find Moses in despair. He has been leading the people of Israel for some time. There have been some great successes, escaping Egypt, crossing the Red Sea, surviving on manna and quail in the desert, but when he goes up Mount Sinai to receive the Law from God, he comes down to find that the Israelites have rejected him and rejected God. He is crushed, telling God that he cannot go on. In the middle of his greatest disappointment and failure, he calls to God, and we might expect that he will ask for wisdom, or strength, or guidance, or perseverance. Instead, he says to God, 'Show me your glory.'*** In

* John 3:16 [emphasis added].
** Zephaniah 3:17.
*** Exodus 33:18.

this moment of weakness and fragility the thing he wanted more than anything else was to see the beauty of God.

All our longings in this life are really a longing for the glory of God. We are drawn to beauty in this world because behind every beautiful thing is God himself. St Augustine said that 'God is the beauty in all things beautiful.' All beauty in the world gives us a glimpse of the truly beautiful one, who is God himself. He is the one who fills all our longings. He's the one who fulfils our desires. Dostoevsky said, 'I believe that there is no one lovelier, deeper, more sympathetic and more perfect that Jesus."

Gift-Love

God's glory explains why we love God with a gift-love: because, above all things, he is worth giving your life for. We are always willing to do things for what we consider to be valuable. People make all kinds of sacrifices for money when they value money, or work long hours for the sake of their careers when they value their careers, or endure great hardships for a cause they believe in. God's glory refers to his infinite value. There are all kinds of things that are great to do. There are all kinds of causes that are worth fighting for. But God is the glorious one, and there is nothing more important and more worth fighting for than Jesus himself. He is glorious and so it creates within us a willingness to do anything for him.

In the final scene of John's Gospel, Peter finds himself face to face with Jesus, knowing that only a few days before he has denied him three times. On that occasion Peter had found himself pushed into a corner and was not willing to risk his life for Jesus, so he denied that he even knew him. Now Jesus looks to restore him and so asks him three times, 'Do you love me?' and each time Peter says, 'Lord, you know that I love you.' Then Jesus says to him, 'When you

---

* Dostoevsky, letter to Mme N.D. Fonvisin, 1854, as quoted in *Letters of Fyodor Michailovitch Dostoevsky to His Family and Friends*, Forgotten Books, 2012, p71.

were younger you dressed yourself and went where you wanted; but when you are old you will stretch out your hands and someone else will dress you and lead you where you do not want to go.' And then it says, 'Jesus said this to indicate the kind of death by which Peter would *glorify* God. Then he said to him, "Follow me."'* Because Peter loves Jesus, he will glorify him through his death. That is the gift-love, where we are willing to do anything for God for the sake of his glory.

Appreciative Love

And God's glory is why we love God with an appreciative love. The appreciative love of God is perhaps the highest of all loves. This is where you forget about yourself and become consumed by God himself for his own sake. The greatest moments in life are often when we are loving with an appreciative love. Playing sport is at its best when you cease to think about whether you are enjoying yourself or whether you are contributing what you want to contribute, you are simply consumed by the game. Work at its best is not spent thinking about your own needs or whether you are doing well or badly, but when you get lost in the tasks you are doing. In relationships the high points are often those when you are not thinking about yourself at all but are enjoying the other person for their own sake. These are the greatest moments in our relationship with God, where we forget about our own desires and fears and insecurities, or our efforts and attempts to serve God, but are simply full of delight for our glorious God.

This is the goal of all things and our final destiny. In the new heaven and new earth, when Jesus comes again, we will not love God with a need-love nor with a gift-love, but with an appreciative love, as we live eternally delighting in the beauty of God.

Our relationship with God tends to start with need-love, as we look to him to meet our human need for hope, peace, and

* John 21:18–19.

comfort. It then progresses to gift-love, as we become willing to give ourselves to God, not for our own benefit, but for his. But we end with appreciative love, by loving God who, above all things, is worthy of love. There is nothing greater than this.

GLORIFYING GOD

When you appreciate something or someone, it is natural to want other people to appreciate them too. This is true of books we enjoy, the films that we love, or the people we love. I have been a Best Man at two weddings, and each time I have been delighted, not just for the honour of that position, but mainly because the Best Man speeches gave me the opportunities to tell lots of people how amazing my best friend and my brother are.

Loving God with an appreciative love naturally means that we want other people to appreciate him too. This is what it means to glorify God. When God glorifies us, it means that he makes us more beautiful, more ourselves, more radiant. When we glorify God, it means enabling people to see God for who he is, in all his beauty and greatness. We can glorify God through what we say or how we live. It can be through success or failure, from things going well or badly, through joys or in heartbreak.

This has been the purpose of this book, that I in writing it, and you in reading it, might see a little more of the beauty of God, knowing his love for you, and loving him in return. That you might love him because you need that love. That you might love him because he is worthy of that love.

Of course, this only scratches the surface. God's love is infinite. It will take eternity to discover it properly and experience it fully. It feels like we have barely begun to talk about Romans or even the love of God in Romans. And it is so much better to experience the love of God than to talk or write about it. My prayer is that each of you would know more fully the glories of God's love.

In the end it is all quite simple. When our youngest daughter Ettie was a few weeks old, one of our other children decided to write a story about her. It simply said this: 'Once apon a time there was Ettie and she was loved.' It is the most perfect story I've ever come across (despite the misspelling of 'upon'). It's the story of your life and my life. And it will go on forever, with each chapter better than the one before.

Muddy
Pearl